MICROSOFT® WORKS 3 FOR WINDOWS®

FOR DUMMIES®

Quick Reference

by Michael J. Partington

IDG BOOKS WORLDWIDE

IDG Books Worldwide, Inc.
An International Data Group Company

Foster City, CA ♦ Chicago, IL ♦ Indianapolis, IN ♦ Braintree, MA ♦ Dallas, TX

Microsoft® Works 3 For Windows® For Dummies® Quick Reference

Published by
IDG Books Worldwide, Inc.
An International Data Group Company
919 E. Hillsdale Blvd.
Suite 400
Foster City, CA 94404

Library of Congress Catalog Card No.: 94-79835

ISBN: 1-56884-959-1

Printed in the United States of America

10 9 8 7 6 5 4 3 2

1A/SU/RQ/ZV

Distributed in the United States by IDG Books Worldwide, Inc.

Distributed by Macmillan Canada for Canada; by Computer and Technical Books for the Caribbean Basin; by Contemporanea de Ediciones for Venezuela; by Distribuidora Cuspide for Argentina; by CITEC for Brazil; by Ediciones ZETA S.C.R. Ltda. for Peru; by Editorial Limusa SA for Mexico; by Transworld Publishers Limited in the United Kingdom and Europe; by Al-Maiman Publishers & Distributors for Saudi Arabia; by Simron Pty. Ltd. for South Africa; by IDG Communications (HK) Ltd. for Hong Kong; by Toppan Company Ltd. for Japan; by Addison Wesley Publishing Company for Korea; by Longman Singapore Publishers Ltd. for Singapore, Malaysia, Thailand, and Indonesia; by Unalis Corporation for Taiwan; by WS Computer Publishing Company, Inc. for the Philippines; by WoodsLane Pty. Ltd. for Australia; by WoodsLane Enterprises Ltd. for New Zealand.

For general information on IDG Books Worldwide's books in the U.S., please call our Consumer Customer Service department at 800-762-2974. For reseller information, including discounts and premium sales, please call our Reseller Customer Service department at 800-434-3422.

For information on where to purchase IDG Books Worldwide's books outside the U.S., contact IDG Books Worldwide at 415-655-3021 or fax 415-655-3295.

For information on translations, contact Marc Jeffrey Mikulich, Director, Foreign & Subsidiary Rights, at IDG Books Worldwide, 415-655-3018 or fax 415-655-3295.

For sales inquiries and special prices for bulk quantities, write to the address above or call IDG Books Worldwide at 415-655-3200.

For information on using IDG Books Worldwide's books in the classroom, or ordering examination copies, contact Jim Kelly at 800-434-2086.

For authorization to photocopy items for corporate, personal, or educational use, please contact Copyright Clearance Center, 222 Rosewood Drive, Danvers, MA 01923, or fax 508-750-4470.

is a trademark under exclusive license to IDG Books Worldwide, Inc., from International Data Group, Inc.

About the Author

Michael Partington is the technical editor of over 25 computer books. He has taught Windows 3.1, Pagemaker, and CorelDraw. As a freelance artist, he uses the power of a computer to help him create fine art, which is shown in many midwestern galleries, lobbies, offices, and museums. When his role switches to a master horologist, Michael uses a computer to inventory the hundreds of tower clock parts he is restoring. As an inventor and manufacturing engineer, Michael uses a computer to create prototype drawings of mechanical innovations and machines. As a father, Michael uses a computer to keep his children entertained while he discusses computers with his wife.

ABOUT IDG BOOKS WORLDWIDE

Welcome to the world of IDG Books Worldwide.

IDG Books Worldwide, Inc., is a subsidiary of International Data Group, the world's largest publisher of computer-related information and the leading global provider of information services on information technology. IDG was founded more than 25 years ago and now employs more than 7,700 people worldwide. IDG publishes more than 250 computer publications in 67 countries (see listing below). More than 70 million people read one or more IDG publications each month.

Launched in 1990, IDG Books Worldwide is today the #1 publisher of best-selling computer books in the United States. We are proud to have received 8 awards from the Computer Press Association in recognition of editorial excellence and three from Computer Currents' First Annual Readers' Choice Awards, and our best-selling *...For Dummies*® series has more than 19 million copies in print with translations in 28 languages. IDG Books Worldwide, through a joint venture with IDG's Hi-Tech Beijing, became the first U.S. publisher to publish a computer book in the People's Republic of China. In record time, IDG Books Worldwide has become the first choice for millions of readers around the world who want to learn how to better manage their businesses.

Our mission is simple: Every one of our books is designed to bring extra value and skill-building instructions to the reader. Our books are written by experts who understand and care about our readers. The knowledge base of our editorial staff comes from years of experience in publishing, education, and journalism — experience which we use to produce books for the '90s. In short, we care about books, so we attract the best people. We devote special attention to details such as audience, interior design, use of icons, and illustrations. And because we use an efficient process of authoring, editing, and desktop publishing our books electronically, we can spend more time ensuring superior content and spend less time on the technicalities of making books.

You can count on our commitment to deliver high-quality books at competitive prices on topics you want to read about. At IDG Books Worldwide, we continue in the IDG tradition of delivering quality for more than 25 years. You'll find no better book on a subject than one from IDG Books Worldwide.

John J. Kilcullen

John Kilcullen
President and CEO
IDG Books Worldwide, Inc.

IDG Books Worldwide, Inc., is a publication of International Data Group, the world's largest publisher of computer-related information and the leading global provider of information services on information technology. International Data Group publishes over 250 computer publications in 67 countries. Seventy million people read one or more International Data Group publications each month. International Data Group's publications include: **ARGENTINA:** Computerworld Argentina, GamePro, Infoworld, PC World Argentina; **AUSTRALIA:** Australian Macworld, Client/Server Journal, Computer Living, Computerworld, Digital Living, Mac World, Publishing Essentials, Reseller, AUSTRIA: Computerwelt, PC TEST; **BELARUS:** PC World Belarus; **BELGIUM:** Data News; **BRAZIL:** Annuário de Informática, Computerworld Brazil, Connections, Super Game Power, Macworld, PC World Brazil, Publish Brazil, SUPERGAME; **BULGARIA:** Computerworld Bulgaria, Networkworld/Bulgaria, PC & MacWorld Bulgaria; **CANADA:** CIO Canada, InfoCanada, Network World Canada, Reseller World; **CHILE:** Computerworld Chile, GamePro, PC World Chile; **COLUMBIA:** Computerworld Colombia, GamePro, PC World Colombia; **COSTA RICA:** PC World Costa Rica/Nicaragua; **THE CZECH AND SLOVAK REPUBLICS:** Computerworld Czechoslovakia, Elektronika Czechoslovakia, PC World Czechoslovakia; **DENMARK:** Communications World, Computerworld Danmark, Macworld Danmark, PC World Danmark, PC World Danmark Supplements, TECH World; **DOMINICAN REPUBLIC:** PC World Republica Dominicana; **ECUADOR:** PC World Ecuador, GamePro; **EGYPT:** Computerworld Middle East, PC World Middle East; **EL SALVADOR:** PC World Central America; **FINLAND:** MikroPC, Tietoverkko, Tietoviikko; **FRANCE:** Distributique, Golden, Info PC, Le Guide du Monde Informatique, Le Monde Informatique, Reseaux & Telecoms; **GERMANY:** Computer Business, Computerwoche, Computerwoche Extra, Computerwoche Focus, Electronic Entertainment, GamePro, I/M Information Management, Macwelt, PC Welt; **GREECE:** GamePro, Macworld & PC World; **GUATEMALA:** PC World Centro America; **HONDURAS:** PC World Centro America; **HONG KONG:** Computerworld Hong Kong, PC World Hong Kong, Publish in Asia; **HUNGARY:** ABCD CD-ROM, Computerworld Szamitastechnika, PC & Mac World Hungary, PC-X Magazine; **INDIA:** Computerworld India, PC World India, Publish in Asia; **INDONESIA:** InfoKomputer PC World, Komputek Computerworld, Publish in Asia; **IRELAND:** ComputerScope, PC Live!; **ISRAEL:** PC World 32 BIT, People & Computers; **ITALY:** Computerworld Italia, Computerworld Italia Special Editions, Lotus Italia, Macworld Italia, Networking Italia, PC Shopping, PC World Italia, PC World/Walt Disney; **JAPAN:** Macworld Japan, Nikkei Personal Computing, SunWorld Japan, Windows World Japan; **KENYA:** East African Computer News; **KOREA:** Hi-Tech Information/Computerworld, Macworld Korea, PC World Korea; **MACEDONIA:** PC World Macedonia; **MALAYSIA:** Computerworld Malaysia, PC World Malaysia, Publish in Asia; **MEXICO:** Computerworld Mexico, GamePro, Macworld, PC World Mexico; **MYANMAR:** PC World Myanmar; **NETHERLANDS:** Computable, Computer! Totaal, LAN Magazine, Macworld, Net Magazine; **NEW ZEALAND:** Computer Buyer, Computerworld New Zealand, MTB, Network World, PC World New Zealand; **NICARAGUA:** PC World Costa Rica/Nicaragua; **NIGERIA:** PC World Africa; **NORWAY:** Computerworld Norge, Computerworld Privat, CW Rapport Klient/Tjener, CW Rapport Nett & Telecom, CW Rapport Offentlig Sektor, IDG's KURSGUIDE, Macworld Norge, Multimedia World, PC World Ekspress, PC World Nett, PC World Norge, PC World's Produktguide, Windows World Spesial; **PAKISTAN:** Computerworld Pakistan, PC World Pakistan; **PANAMA:** GamePro, PC World Panama; **PARAGUAY:** PC World Paraguay; **P. R. OF CHINA:** China Computerworld, China Infoworld, Computer & Communications, Electronic Product World, Electronics Today, Game Camp, PC World China, Popular Computer Week, Software World, Telecom Product World; **PERU:** Computerworld Peru, GamePro, PC World Profesional Peru, PC World Peru; **POLAND:** Computerworld Poland, Computerworld Special Report, Macworld, Networld, PC World Komputer; **PHILIPPINES:** Computerworld Philippines, PC Digest, Publish in Asia; **PORTUGAL:** Cerebro/PC World, Correio Informático/Computerworld, Mac•In/PC•In Portugal; **PUERTO RICO:** PC World Puerto Rico; **ROMANIA:** Computerworld Romania, PC World Romania, Telecom Romania; **RUSSIA:** Computerworld Rossiya, Network World Russia, PC World Russia; **SINGAPORE:** Computerworld Singapore, PC World Singapore, Publish in Asia; **SLOVENIA:** MONITOR; **SOUTH AFRICA:** Computer Mail, S.A., Network World S.A., Software World; **SPAIN:** Computerworld España, COMUNICACIONES WORLD, Dealer World, Macworld España, PC World España; **SWEDEN:** CAP&Design, Computer Sweden, Corporate Computing, MacWorld, Maxi Data, MikroDatorn, Natverk & Kommunikation, PC/Aktiv, PC World, Windows World; **SWITZERLAND:** Computerworld Schweiz, Macworld Schweiz, PCtip; **TAIWAN:** Computerworld Taiwan, Macworld Taiwan, PC World Taiwan, Publish in Asia, Windows World; **THAILAND:** Thai Computerworld, Publish in Asia; **TURKEY:** Computerworld Monitör, Macworld Türkiye, PC WORLD Turkiye; **UKRAINE:** Computerworld Kiev, Computer Software Magazine, PC World Ukraine; **UNITED KINGDOM:** Acorn User, Amiga Computing, Amiga Action, Apple talk, CD Focus, CD-ROM Now, Computing, Connexion, GamePro, Lotus Magazine, Macaction, Macworld, Open Computing, Parents and Computers, PC Home, PC Works, The WEB; **UNITED STATES:** Cable in the Classroom, CD Review, CIO Magazine, Computerworld, Computer Retail Week, Client/Server Journal, Digital Video Magazine, DOS World, Electronic, InfoWorld, I-Way, Macworld, Maximize, MULTIMEDIA WORLD, Network World, PC World, PUBLISH, SWATPro Magazine, Video Event, WebMaster; **URUGUAY:** PC World Uruguay; **VENEZUELA:** Computerworld Venezuela, GamePro, PC World Venezuela; and **VIETNAM:** PC World Vietnam

Acknowledgments

Special thanks to Diane Steele for her faith and trust in me, to Tim Gallan for this project's structure and guidance, to Jennifer Wallis for her editing skills, and to Ray Werner for being my technical watchdog.

(The publisher would like to give special thanks to Patrick J. McGovern, without whom this book would not have been possible.)

Dedication

Thanks to my wife, Marta. Without her, I'd still be a computer dummy.

Credits

Senior Vice President and Publisher
Milissa L. Koloski

Associate Publisher
Diane Graves Steele

Brand Manager
Judith A. Taylor

Editorial Managers
Kristin A. Cocks
Mary Corder

Product Development Manager
Mary Bednarek

Editorial Executive Assistant
Richard Graves

Editorial Assistants
Constance Carlisle
Chris Collins
Stacey Holden Prince
Kevin Spencer

Acquisitions Assistant
Suki Gear

Production Director
Beth Jenkins

Supervisor of Project Coordination
Cindy L. Phipps

Supervisor of Page Layout
Kathie S. Schnorr

Pre-Press Coordination
Steve Peake
Tony Augsburger
Patricia R. Reynolds
Theresa Sánchez-Baker
Elizabeth Cárdenas-Nelson

Media/Archive Coordination
Paul Belcastro
Leslie Popplewell

Associate Project Editor
A. Timothy Gallan

Copy Editor
Jennifer J. Wallis

Technical Reviewer
Ray Werner

Project Coordinator
Valery Bourke

Graphics Coordination
Shelley Lea
Gina Scott
Carla Radzikinas

Production Page Layout
Chris Collins

Proofreaders
Jennifer Kaufeld
Dwight Ramsey

Indexer
Sherry Massey

Cover Design
Kavish + Kavish

Contents at a Glance

Are you a new computer user — an authentic computer dummy? (And when I say "dummy," I'm not commenting on your intelligence; it's just that technology sometimes makes us feel as though we're dummies.) Just think: fifteen years ago, your computer and software would have fetched two and a half or three million dollars from a major computer-using corporation. So there's really nothing wrong with turning to a resource like this book for information and help. Sure, using Works may sound like a lot of work, but don't be intimidated — just read on.

Finding your way through the maze

Each part of this book has its own method of showing you the Windows and Works commands. The following explains what each method is and when to use them.

- The Introduction gives you a run-through of some of the basic terms and concepts used throughout the book. It covers everything from mouse dragging and dropping (not droppings) to window bars (adults only). This section will get you started on the right track.

- Part I, "How Works Works," treats you to an overview of the program. Here you learn what each accessory of Works is used for. You see exactly how to access the six Works accessories while actually working in the Works program. Don't know what an accessory looks like? Look here for that, too.

  OK, so you may need a tad more advice. If you want the complete Works start-up kit, check out some other *For Dummies* books: *DOS For Dummies, Windows For Dummies,* and *Microsoft Works 3 For Windows For Dummies.*

- Part II, "The Works Commands," lists the most commonly used Works commands in alphabetical order — complete with which keys you press to access those commands. At the end of each listing, look for some extra tidbits about the command, along with references to other Works commands listed in this book. In Part II you find just enough information to get started, but not so much that you get confused.

- Part III, "A Toolbar Cross-Reference," gives you exactly what you expect to get from a part with such a boring name. You see pictures of the complete toolbar for each part of Works, along with each toolbar button's icon and a description of what the button does — thrown in for good measure.

- Part IV, "The Glossary," is, well, it's just your basic glossary with definitions for terms that you might not be familiar with. Hey, here's a helpful feature: look for words in *italics* throughout the book; you can find their definitions in the glossary.

- Use the Index to quickly look up that one-and-only feature of Works that you don't know about (or maybe forgot about, or maybe could care less about).

Using the Alt key combos

The following scenario is designed with the foolhardy in mind:

Imagine that time is running out on an important project deadline. Unfortunately, the aforementioned project is spread out over five different windows on your computer screen. Even more unfortunately, you have only 30 minutes left to check the spelling, save, and print the project before your job is in jeopardy.

Suddenly, your mouse bites the dust. *Oh, no!* What do you do? First, bury it. (A word of advice: Don't wait too long for a sympathy card from Bill Gates). Second, don't despair — all is not lost. Those people at Microsoft thought of everything. All of the commands in Works and Windows can also be accessed by using a few simple keystrokes. I know, you're probably saying to yourself: "Yeah, right. How can anyone learn a zillion keystrokes and use them to finish a complex project in only 30 minutes?" No problem, because all of the Windows commands and all of its installed programs' commands (including Works') are right in front of your face. They're called the *Alt key combos*.

Taking your first Alt trip

The Alt key combos are made up of two keystrokes. Press the Alt key on your keyboard and then press and release a character key. That's it. You've successfully completed the Alt key combo. You can now go a step further.

All menus and dialog boxes in Windows have words that contain some underlined letters. These underlined letters are half of the Alt key combo. You provide the other half. Here are the easy steps to carrying out a command using the Alt key combo:

1. Look in your program for the underlined letter of the command or option that you want to carry out.

   Open Works or any other program in Windows, and you see the <u>F</u>ile menu in the upper left corner of the program window.

2. Press the Alt key on your keyboard.

3. Press the letter or number that is underlined in your application's command or option.

For example, if you press F on your keyboard, the <u>F</u>ile menu drops down.

4. If you see any other underlined character listed (for options or commands), press that character key on your keyboard.

For example, in the <u>F</u>ile menu, the first two commands will be the <u>N</u>ew and <u>O</u>pen commands. You can press one of the underlined letters to perform its command.

Here's how I show the menu commands in this book. For the preceding steps, the book's command structure looks like this:

<u>F</u>ile⇨<u>N</u>ew

or

<u>F</u>ile⇨<u>O</u>pen

The underlined letters are those used with the Alt key combos. The right-pointing arrow shows that the command (on the right) is on the menu (on the left). So if I were to say "Choose <u>F</u>ile⇨<u>O</u>pen," I mean "Choose the Open command from the File menu." To illustrate the equivalent keyboard shortcuts for commands, I use the following conventions:

Alt+F,N

or

Alt+F,O

The plus sign means that when both pair of keys are pressed, a menu drops from the menu bar. The comma separates the first keystroke from a second one. Notice that in this case (Alt + menu keystroke, command keystroke), you don't really need to hold down the Alt key with the menu keystroke or the command keystroke. But if you do, that's okay; it will still work.

Of course, to avoid using Alt key combos, just use your mouse.

The Must-Know Terms

If you're a rank beginner with the Works program running in the Windows environment, then you need to read the following descriptions to help you understand some of this book's computer jargon. First, you read about the mouse movements. Next, you see more keyboard stuff along with descriptions of the various window parts that all Windows programs share. Finally, you stumble upon some beginning tips about the workings and wonders of Windows.

Mouse movements

It's time to tell you just what that mouse can do. If you think you use a mouse by just moving it with your hand and pressing a button with a finger — you're right. But you'd better read about this mouse motion stuff anyway, because it's *how* you move that hand and press that finger that really counts.

Pointing

Pointing means that you move your mouse so that your *screen cursor* moves to the spot you want in a program.

Clicking

Clicking means that you press the left mouse button and then release it (named after the clicking sound the mouse makes). *Right-clicking* is when you press the right mouse button and then release it. Duh!

Dragging

Dragging means that you click or select something and then move it around in the program by moving the mouse while still pressing the left mouse button.

Dragging and dropping

Dragging and dropping means that you drag something and then release the left mouse button — usually dropping your selection into another area of the program's document window or into a different application's window.

Double-clicking

Double-clicking means that you press the left mouse button twice in rapid succession. *Triple-clicking* is when you press the left mouse button three times in rapid succession. *Quadruple-clicking* is a good mouse exercise.

Selecting with a marquee

Selecting with a marquee (only available in certain programs) means that you drag the mouse, and by doing so, you draw a rectangular lasso on the screen. Anything inside the lasso becomes selected. This feature got its name because after you draw the dotted-lined lasso with your mouse, it moves like an old movie theater sign — or marquee.

Key keystrokes

Beginning users of a Windows program tend to use the mouse to choose commands from the menus. This is good news, because anyone can quickly get started in an unfamiliar program. As first-time users become accustomed to the program's frequently used commands, they start to use keystroke combinations instead. Doing so saves time because one hand isn't going back and forth from keyboard to mouse.

Hot key combos

If you look at any drop-down menu from the menu bar, you see those underlined Alt keys I talked about earlier. To the right of some of the menu's commands you see the other type of key-stroke combination, the *hot key* combo. These key stroke combinations can use the Ctrl keys, the Shift keys, or sometimes a function key (like F12).

When you press a hot key combo, you can perform the command without the use of the menu bar. Your work is much easier if you memorize some of them. After all, if you always go into a drop-down menu to find the hot key combo, you may as well use the Alt key combos or just click the command with your mouse.

Here's an example:

File⇨New (the menu command)

is the same as

Alt+F,N (the Alt key combo)

is the same as

Crtl+N (the hot key combo)

Ellipses

When you look at any drop-down menu, you see the program's commands. Directly following some of these commands, you see a series of three dots, called an *ellipsis*. Selecting a command with an ellipsis suffix always brings up a dialog box in your program's window. You can close an unwanted dialog box by pressing Esc.

Windows parts inventory

Different areas of a Windows window perform many various tasks. If you learn them once, you'll be able to use them from any window in any program. The consistency of the interface is what makes Microsoft Windows a very popular computer working environment.

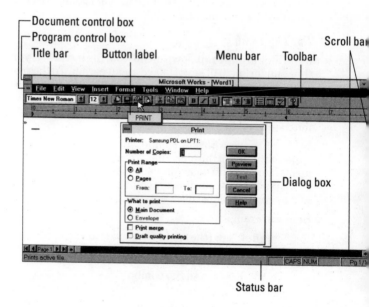

Title bar

The *title bar* is the horizontal bar — usually containing a title — at the top of any window, dialog box, program, or working document. Dragging the title bar will move the window.

Menu bar

The *menu bar* is the horizontal bar that contains the menu titles. When you click one of the menu bar's titles, a drop-down menu appears, allowing you to select a menu command. The menu bar is the second bar from the top in Works.

Toolbar, toolbar buttons, and button labels

The *toolbar* lies under the menu bar, which makes it the third bar from the top. The toolbar is easy to recognize because it's filled with a variety of colored *toolbar buttons*. These buttons replicate most of the menu bar's commands, Alt key combos, and hot key combos. Pointing to a toolbar button with your mouse pointer will make the button show its *button label*. The button label carries the same name as the menu command that the button replicates. Clicking a button in the toolbar carries out the button's command. The equivalent menu command of a button might bring up a dialog box, but clicking the button usually performs an action, which often makes clicking buttons on the toolbar faster than choosing commands from menus.

Scroll bars

Scroll bars are the bars that appear on the right and bottom sides of a window when the contents of the window are larger than your computer screen. These funny-looking elevators play a handy role in moving you around to see the hidden portions of your document. Scroll bars consist of a *scroll box* (the elevator), an *elevator shaft* (what the scroll box moves around in), and two *scroll arrows* (on each end of the elevator shaft) which point in opposite directions. You can click one of the scroll arrows to move around a window in small increments, or you can drag and drop the scroll box to move around a window in large increments. If you click in an empty part of the elevator shaft (between a scroll arrow and the scroll box), you move a full screen page for each mouse click. You can read more about scroll bars in Chapter 6 of *Windows For Dummies*.

Control box and its menu

Every window in Windows and therefore in Works has a *control box*. This small button-like box looks like the drawer of a filing cabinet and is located at the top-left corner of every open window. Double-clicking it closes the current window. If you close your program window by double-clicking the control box and you have not saved your work file, a warning dialog box reminds you to do so. If you click the *control box* only once, a list of commands opens. See *Windows For Dummies* for more stuff you can do with windows and their control boxes.

Status bar

Some programs display information about a file in an area called the *status bar*. The status bar is usually displayed at the bottom of your open program's window, and it provides you with such information as mouse position, page number, text color, and command prompts.

Dialog box

A *dialog box* is the box that opens when you select a command that is followed by an ellipsis from the menu bar. Dialog boxes appear in your program so that more information, options, and data can be added or changed, thus affecting how the command functions. These additional dialog box options make the command customizable. Good dialog boxes are the building blocks of a concise and easy-to-use program.

Defaults

The *default settings* — or just *defaults* — are the initial settings of the software. These settings are displayed in dialog boxes, menus, and pop-up menus. If you're not sure about choosing an option in a dialog box, the best thing to do is nothing — just leave all settings at their default. When a manual or book tells you to keep the default settings, don't change them.

Part 1

How Works Works

The Main Parts

The Works program is really a simple program, but it can seem complicated unless you are aware that it is divided into several parts: a word processor, a spreadsheet with a charting program, a database, and communications software. This book shows you how to enter data into the *database*, take it into the *spreadsheet*, turn the spreadsheet's data results into a *chart*, paste the chart into a letter inside the *word processor*, and send that letter out with the *modem*.

The Startup dialog box

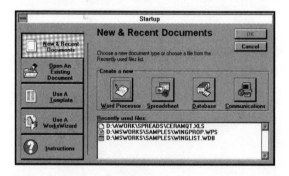

You find the *Startup dialog box* in the first screen of the Works program. This is your jumping-off point each time you open the program. Simply click a button in the Create a new section of the Startup dialog box to begin a new document in Works. You can always get back to this dialog box from anywhere in the Works program by clicking the Startup Dialog button in the toolbar.

The word processor

You will probably use Works' word processor more often than any of its other applications. Its friendly, graphical interface and well-structured menus make it easy for you to create and edit a wide variety of documents. Think of this word processor as the core of the Works program: it can incorporate graphics and information from the database, spreadsheet, ClipArt Gallery, and modem. When you combine all these various elements into a word-processing document, you look like a great digital virtuoso.

The spreadsheet and spreadsheet charting

Remember your math teacher in school demanding "Show all your work!" Well, a spreadsheet is kind of the same way. The first time you create a spreadsheet, you need to create math formulas for the spreadsheet to use. After you do that, you can use the sheet again and again without refiguring and showing all the formulas. You can also create all kinds of charts that demonstrate the results of your spreadsheet and place them in your Works documents.

The database and database reporting

You may have heard a novice computer user say, "Gee whiz, I can keep all my recipes on my computer now — and sort them into categories!" That's true, a database will do this for you — but you can do a lot more with the database, too. Just think of your excitement as you search for that special Grateful Dead bootleg recording from amongst the hundreds in your LP recording database. Also, don't forget that you can create a mailing database report for Thursday night's bowling league members. You'll be more popular than a 300 game.

Communications

You must have a modem in order to use the communications part of the Works program. A modem is an electronic device that connects your computer to a telephone line. Having a modem along with the Works communication program allows you to connect to any other computer on earth, as long as it also has a modem. Now your Works documents can be sent around the world at the speed of light. Way cool!

More Startup options

On the left side of the Startup dialog box is a list of other startup options. By default, the New & Recent Documents button is selected. You can tell it's selected by the way the button looks — it appears to be pressed in.

When you click the second button—Open An Existing Document— you bring up the Open dialog box. From here you can select Works files from your computer's disks.

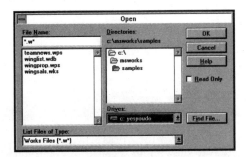

The third button in the column, Use A Template, can be clicked when you want to create a new document. A *template* is a document with a lot of the styles, designs, and layouts already inserted for you. What a work-saver!

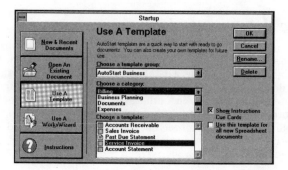

The fourth button in the column is the Use A WorksWizard button. Click it, make your selection from the Choose a WorksWizard list, and then answer the dialog box questions that follow. Using your answers and some of its built-in templates, the WorksWizard quickly comes up with some nicely prepared and styled documents — with most of the work finished for you.

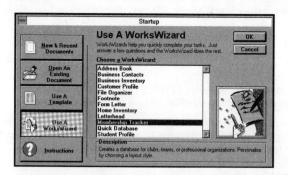

The aptly named Instructions button provides, you guessed it, additional instructions for the first four buttons in the Startup dialog box.

The Accessories

Hidden in the applications of the Works program are six accessories that are handy to know about because they help you with those added touches when you prepare that special document. You can find a brief description of each of them below.

If you need more detailed information about these accessories, see *Microsoft Works 3 For Windows For Dummies*.

Note-It

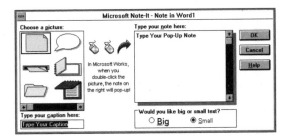

The *Note-It* program emulates those yellow stick-it notes that your office buys millions of, except that these are the electronic kind. Any time you need to make a note to yourself while using the database or the word processor, just use Works' Note-It program to stick that note on your document without interfering with the structure or the contents of your document. The Note-It command is in the Insert menu of the database form and the word processor.

ClipArt Gallery

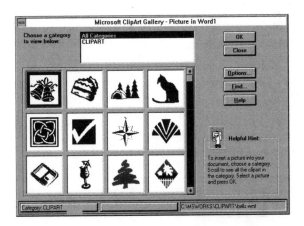

The ClipArt Gallery is a nice little accessory that shows you — in *thumbnail* form — all the pictures, artwork, and clip art on your hard drive. This feature makes it easy to locate those fancy graphics and insert them into your word processing document or database form. The ClipArt command is in the Insert menu of the database form and the word processor. After the Gallery is open, you can even categorize the library of images with the Gallery's special menu bar.

WordArt

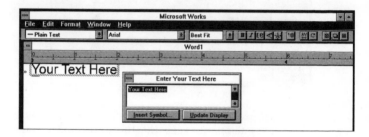

WordArt gives any letter, word, or sentence in your document a customized look. You can be your own typographer and shape characters into special headlines, titles, or logos. The WordArt command is in the Insert menu of the database form and the word processor. When WordArt is open, you can use special tools in its toolbar.

Microsoft Draw

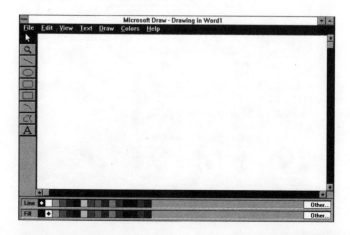

Can't find the clip art that you need from the ClipArt Gallery? Just draw your own art with Microsoft Draw. This is a special *drawing program* that allows you to create your own artwork. This custom art program allows you to size your drawings as large as you want without creating those funny jagged edges — unlike those paintings found in the Microsoft Paint painting program. You can find the Drawing command in two places: either in the Insert menu in a database form or in the Insert menu in the word processor. You can choose either command to open the Microsoft Draw program. A special menu bar, toolbar, and window appear when you work in Microsoft Draw.

Electronic mail

The Send command in the File menu of the database, spreadsheet, and word processor sends the document that is currently open through Microsoft Mail (if you are connected to a *network*). If you're not on a network, you can send mail *(electronic mail)* as whole documents or as text messages with the Works Communications program.

The chart accessory

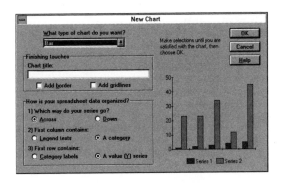

Inside the spreadsheet is a nifty accessory that takes your selected data and turns it into a cool-looking chart of your choice. Just click the New Chart toolbar button and you see a dialog box with lots of options that customize the new chart. After a chart is created, it can be inserted into a word processing document or a data form.

The spell checker

The spell checker is the easiest way to look up misspelled words in your document. After you have completed your document, you can run the spell checker and it will stop and highlight any word that is not in its built-in electronic dictionary. This electronic dictionary holds more than 110,000 words. When you use the spell checker, special words can be added to the dictionary, such as last names, technical jargon, and stuff that a regular dictionary doesn't list. The Spelling command is in the Tools menu of the database, spreadsheet, and word processor, or you can simply click the Spelling button in the word processor's toolbar.

Part II

The Works Commands

What Are Those Round Symbols for, Anyway?

Those round symbols (icons) you see throughout Part II show you the level of difficulty of each Works command. The easiest commands have a Thumbs Up icon, while the hardest commands have the For Gurus Only icon. The following defines each icon so that you can decide exactly what command you want to try (or avoid).

The user icons

After each command name, the user icons show you the difficulty level of that command, letting you learn at your own pace.

 For the Average User icon. This icon reassures you that this is a good command to use if you are an average user of Works.

 Not For the Average User icon. This icon lets you know that the command should be avoided if you are an average user of Works.

 Might Be For the Average User icon. This icon lets you know that the command may be worth learning if you are an average user of Works.

The command rating icons

The *command rating* icons, which follow the command name, give you a clue about how easy it is for you to successfully use this command.

 Safe icon. The command is very safe to use if this icon is present.

 Be Careful icon. Be careful and read slowly when you see this icon.

 Some Danger icon. This icon warns you to study the command carefully before using it.

For Gurus Only icon. The experts swarm to feed on these icons — and you should let them!

The extra info icons

Extra info icons appear next to the extra information that this book gives about each command. These icons advise you about the contents of that information and help you skim through the boring stuff faster.

Warning icon. This icon points out extra warning information that you should read about the command.

Tip icon. Look for these everywhere — they contain some mighty fine tips and shortcuts to using the Works program.

Remember icon. Watch for this icon. It contains information to remind you about some other aspects of Works that you've read — or should read, if you have skipped around this book.

Reference icon. This icon appears next to references to associated commands in this book.

Cross-Reference icon. This icon appears next to cross-references to expanded information in *Microsoft Works 3 For Windows For Dummies,* also published by IDG Books.

Edit⇨Clear

This command deletes the selected item or items.

Hot key hysteria

Ample info

The Clear command wipes out anything that is selected. Pressing Delete is the fastest way to accomplish the same task.

Extra info

If you're overly ambitious and delete parts of your work by mistake, don't forget the Ctrl+Z key combination (Edit⇨Undo) to undo your error.

Some users of Windows use the Edit⇨Cut command to clear stuff from their documents. Although this seems to work fine, it should be avoided — using Cut fills the Windows Clipboard and robs the system of memory that could be used to run other programs.

Edit⇨Clear Field Entry

This command deletes a field entry in a Works database while in the *list view*, *query view*, or *form view*.

Extra info

Pressing Delete, instead of using the command, doesn't work here.

Check out the View⇨List, View⇨Query, and View⇨Form (F9) database commands.

Edit⇨Copy

Copies the selected item(s) and puts the copy in the Windows Clipboard.

Minimum mouse motion

Hot key hysteria

Ctrl + **C**

Ample info

You must select (highlight) something before the Copy command is available in the Edit menu. After the selection is copied, the contents go to the Window's Clipboard. If something else is copied, the newest copied contents replace any older contents already in the Clipboard.

Extra info

An easier way to Edit⇨Copy or Edit⇨Paste contents for a short move across your document is to highlight the text that you want to copy or paste, and then, using your mouse, drag that text to its destination while pressing Ctrl. Finally, release the mouse button first and then release the Ctrl key.

The Edit⇨Paste or Edit⇨Paste Special command takes the Clipboard contents and inserts them in your document, spreadsheet, or database.

See *Windows 3.1 For Dummies, 2nd Edition* for more information about selecting and highlighting.

Edit⇨Copy Record

This command copies an entire record from the database form view.

Hot key hysteria

Ctrl + **Shift** + **C**

Ample info

In the database form view, go to the record that you want to copy. Select Copy Record from the Edit menu, which puts a copy of the record in the Windows Clipboard. Move to the record in the database that you want to copy the information to. Choose Paste from the Edit menu and the entire record is copied.

Extra info

You can open another Works document or Windows application and paste a record into it from the Windows Clipboard.

You need the <u>E</u>dit▷<u>P</u>aste command to complete the <u>E</u>dit▷Copy Record command's job.

<u>E</u>dit▷<u>C</u>opy Text

This communications program command works the same way as the regular Windows <u>C</u>opy command, but this one can only copy text to the Clipboard.

Minimum mouse motion

Hot key hysteria

$$\boxed{Ctrl} + \boxed{C}$$

<u>E</u>dit▷Cu<u>t</u>

This command cuts the selected item(s) and puts it on the Windows Clipboard.

Minimum mouse motion

Hot key hysteria

$$\boxed{Ctrl} + \boxed{X}$$

Ample info

You must select (highlight) something for the Cut command to become available in the Edit menu. Once the text is cut, it goes to the Windows Clipboard. If other text is cut later, the most recently cut text replaces the Clipboard's previous contents.

Extra info

An easier way to Cut and Paste contents for a short move across your document is to highlight the text you want to cut, drag it with your mouse, and then release the mouse button when you've reached the desired location.

The Edit⟹Paste or the Edit⟹Paste Special command inserts the Clipboard contents into your document, spreadsheet, or database.

You can always undo a bad cut by pressing Ctrl+Z.

Edit⟹Cut Record

This command cuts an entire record from the database form view.

Hot key hysteria

$$\boxed{Ctrl} + \boxed{Shift} + \boxed{X}$$

Extra info

The Edit⟹Cut Record command cuts a record to the Clipboard, and the Edit⟹Copy Record copies a record to the Clipboard. Duh. See the Edit⟹Copy Record command for information about copying a record.

Edit⟹Data Labels

This command inserts data labels into the chart next to the plotted graphic that they represent. This command creates, changes, or deletes the data labels on a chart created by the Works spreadsheet charting program.

Ample info

You can make changes to data labels from two different Data Labels dialog boxes. The first dialog box appears when you edit a bar or a line chart, and the second type is displayed when you work with a pie chart.

You can use a bar or line chart's plotted graphic values as the data labels by checking the Use series data option in the dialog box and then clicking OK or pressing Enter.

To delete or edit the data labels in a line or bar chart, make sure the Use series data option is unchecked and change or delete the labels in the 1st, 2nd, 3rd, and so on, text boxes. Click OK or press Enter to complete the process.

To add spreadsheet information as data labels in a line or bar chart, first copy the cell's data to the Clipboard (Ctrl+C), summon Data Labels from the Edit menu, make sure that the Use series data option is unchecked, and click the Paste button in the dialog box. Click OK or press Enter to complete the process.

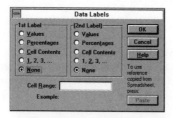

You can use a pie chart's plotted graphic values as the data labels by checking the Use series data option in the dialog box and then clicking OK or pressing the Enter key.

To add data labels to a pie chart, click to choose Values, Percentages, Cell Contents, or 1,2,3 from the first, second, or both option lists, and then click OK or press the Enter key.

To delete the data labels from a pie chart, select None as the 1st Label and 2nd Label option and click OK or press the Enter key.

To add spreadsheet information as data labels in a pie chart, first copy a cell range containing the labels from your spreadsheet to the Clipboard (Ctrl+C), summon Data Labels from the Edit menu, and click the Paste button in the Data Labels dialog box. The Cell Range text box is then pasted with the copied cell range from the Clipboard. Click OK or press Enter to finish the task.

Extra info

You must first create a spreadsheet chart before you can use the Edit⇨Data Labels command.

The Tools⇨Create New Chart command builds a chart from Works spreadsheet cell data.

Edit⇨Field Name

This command displays the Field Name dialog box where you can enter or change the field column's name in the List view of a Works database document.

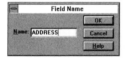

Extra info

You do not have to highlight the entire field column to use this command. Simply highlight one cell from the field column that you want to name or rename.

To display the List view of a database, use the View⇨List command in the database program.

See Chapter 15 in *Microsoft Works 3 For Windows For Dummies* to learn how to create your first database.

Edit⇨Fill Down

This command copies one cell's data contents into every cell that follows it in a highlighted column of a spreadsheet — provided that the cell containing the data you want copied is the first (top) cell of the highlighted column.

Extra info

This command is a lot faster than the Edit⇨Copy command. Use it when you need to fill a long column of cells with the same data.

Edit⇨Fill Right

This command copies one cell's data contents to all the high-lighted cells to the right of it in a spreadsheet's row — provided that the cell with the data to be copied is the first (left) cell of the highlighted cells in the row.

Extra info

This command is a lot faster than the Edit⇨Copy command. Use it when you need to fill a long row of cells with the same data.

Edit⇨Fill Series

This command creates a number or date *series* of a cell's data contents down or across the spreadsheet's highlighted cells — provided that the first cell of the highlighted cells (the left one for a row selection or the top one for a column selection) contains the series' starting value.

If you want to enter data (either numbers or dates) that follow a pattern — like July 4th, July 5th, July 6th, July 7th, and so on — the Fill Series command makes it easy. First, type the series'

beginning number or date in the cell where you want your series to begin (leftmost for row, top for column). Highlight this first cell along with all the other contiguous cells that you want the series to fill. Choose Fill Series from the Edit menu. Next, choose the appropriate type of series from the Units list in the Fill Series dialog box. In the Step by box, enter the number of increments that you want your series to go by (for example, if you want your series to skip every other unit, enter 2). Finally, click OK or press Enter to create your series.

Extra info

The date series starting cell value must be in the following format: 7/9/53 or 7/53 or just July

Dashes or periods for the date's separators do not work.

If you enter a negative number in the Step by box of the Fill Series dialog box, you create a decreasing series.

Edit⇨Find

This command opens the Find dialog box, where you can type text to find within a word processor document or database list, or type the formulas or values to find within the cells of a spreadsheet.

Ample info

In a Works document, enter the text, value, or formula that you want to find in the Find What box.

If you want to look for only the whole word in a word processor document, click Match Whole Word Only to select that option. This option prevents Works from finding text within words. For example, if you're looking for the word "rat," the Find command skips over words such as "inspiration," "separation," and "rattle." You can also find text that specifically matches the case (upper-case or lowercase) of the text you enter by clicking the Match Case option from the Find dialog box.

For example, if the text that you want to find has an uppercase letter, such as "Because," then the Find command only stops on the word when it is capitalized (like at the beginning of a sentence).

After you choose your options from the Find dialog box, click the Find Next button to start the search. Works highlights the first occurrence of the text in the word, spreadsheet, or database document. Keep clicking the Find Next button to continue your search. When you reach the end of the document, Works tells you in an information box. You can click the Cancel button in the dialog box or press Esc to quit the Find command at any time.

Extra info

If you want to find certain text in a word processor document, spreadsheet, or database list and then replace it with different text, see the Edit⇨Replace command.

When the text is found and highlighted during a search, press any key to delete the highlighted text and replace it with whatever you typed.

Edit⇨Go To

This command opens the Go To dialog box. From this dialog box you can quickly get to other places (*bookmarks* in a word processor document, *field names* in a database, and *range names* in a spreadsheet) in Works without scrolling through the document again and again.

Hot key hysteria

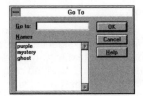

Minimum mouse motion

Double-clicking on the Page Number box in the status bar of a word processor document will open the Find dialog box.

Ample info

The easiest and fastest way to use the Go To dialog box is to double-click a bookmark from a word processor document, a field name from a database, or a range name from a spreadsheet in the Names box. If the list of names is numerous, use the scroll bar to find the name from the list and then double-click it. When you need to go to another spot, press F5 and double-click another name in the Names list.

Extra info

You must insert *bookmarks* in your document, *field names* in your database, or *range names* in your spreadsheet before you can go to anything.

Check out the Insert⇨Bookmark Name, Insert⇨Range Name, and the Insert⇨Record/Field commands first.

Edit⇨Legend/Series Labels

With the Legend/Series Labels command of the Edit menu, you can create, change, or delete a legend from a line chart or bar chart in the Works spreadsheet charting program.

Ample info

Legends are located at the bottom of the chart. They show what the color, fill, and line styles represent in your line chart or bar chart.

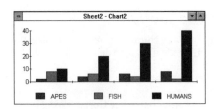

From the Legend/Series Labels dialog box, you can type a name
for each series of the chart in the Value Series boxes. By selecting
the Use a legend radio button, the names from the Value Series
boxes are used as your chart's legend labels. To delete the chart's
legends, delete, uncheck, and deselect everything in the Legend/
Series Labels dialog box. Click OK or press Enter to apply your
options to the chart.

Extra info

You can create the legends for a chart by typing the legend
names in the first column of a spreadsheet, selecting the legends
along with the cells (range) that contains the data, and then
clicking the New Chart button in the spreadsheet toolbar.

You must create a spreadsheet chart before you can use the
Edit⇨Data Labels command.

The Tools⇨Create New Chart command builds a chart from the
spreadsheet's cell data.

Edit⇨Links

This command opens the Links dialog box where you choose
which inserted objects in a Works document you want linked. If a
document's object is linked, it can be double-clicked in the
document to open the Windows program that created it. Also, if
an inserted object is linked, any later changes made to the
object's file by another program are reflected in the inserted
object when the Works document is viewed later.

Ample info

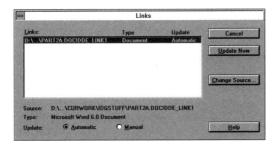

In the Links dialog box you can

- Click the link you want to edit in the Links box.

- Select the type of updating that you want for the selected link by clicking the Automatic or Manual radio button.

- Change the source or location of the linked file by clicking the Change Source button.

- Update manually by clicking the Update Now button.

Extra info

Creating and using links can use up lots of computer system memory. Not having enough memory causes Windows to come to a screeching halt — maybe even to crash. Make sure that your machine has at least 8MB of system RAM before messing with this link stuff.

Thou must first create before thou can edit.

To create a link, see the Insert⇨Object command.

Edit⇨Object

With this command, you can edit an *embedded* or *linked* object in the word processor program and the database form view.

Minimum mouse motion

You can double-click the object in your document to edit it.

Ample info

Select the linked or embedded object in your form or document. Choose the Object command from the Edit menu. This action opens the original program that created the object, along with the object's file. Make the necessary changes to the object and then close the object's creator program. Your form or document is updated with the edited object.

Extra info

Thou must first create before thou can edit.

Check out the Edit⇨Paste Special command along with the Insert⇨Object command and all the other commands at the lower section of the Insert menu.

Creating and using links can use up lots of system memory. Not having enough memory causes Windows to come to a screeching halt.

Edit⇨Paste

This command pastes the contents of the Windows Clipboard into your document at the positon of the cursor.

Minimum mouse motion

Hot key hysteria

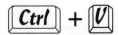

Ample info

Use the Edit⇨Cut or the Edit⇨Copy command to take a selected area of a document to the Clipboard. Position the cursor in your document where you want the Clipboard contents to be pasted and then choose Paste from the Edit menu.

The Edit⇨Paste command is used more often than any other command in all Windows programs. I wish I could write more about it to make it appear more important.

Extra info

If you select something in your document and then use the Edit⇨Paste command, your selection is replaced by the contents of the Clipboard.

You can undo a bad paste job with the Edit⇨Undo (Ctrl+Z) command.

Before the Edit⇨Paste command can work, the contents of the Windows Clipboard must be filled by using Edit⇨Copy or Edit⇨Cut first. The Edit⇨Paste Special command gives you a dialog box full of paste options.

Edit⇨Paste Series

This command opens the Paste Series dialog box to give you a choice of which series in the current spreadsheet's chart you want to paste the Windows Clipboard's data into.

Hot key hysteria

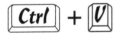

Ample info

In order to use the Paste Series command, you must first select a row or column of cells that contain data from a Works spreadsheet and click the Copy or Cut button from the toolbar. Create a chart with the New Chart button in the toolbar of the spreadsheet or charting accessory—you can also choose the Chart command from the View menu to paste a new series into an old chart.

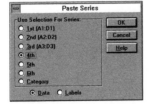

Choose <u>P</u>aste Series from the <u>E</u>dit menu to open the Paste Series dialog box. Now you can click the number of the series that you want the Clipboard's contents pasted to and choose <u>D</u>ata to paste to the data area on the chart, or choose <u>L</u>abels to paste to the label area on the chart.

Extra info

If you use the <u>E</u>dit⇨<u>C</u>opy and the <u>E</u>dit⇨<u>P</u>aste Series command together, as described in the previous paragraph, you can quickly insert series and labels into a chart — just copy information from anywhere in a spreadsheet, database, or document.

<u>E</u>dit⇨<u>P</u>aste <u>S</u>pecial

This command brings up the Paste Special dialog box, which gives you pasting options to choose from before pasting the contents of the Clipboard into your document.

Ample info

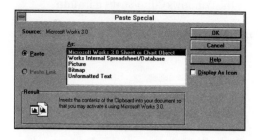

From the Paste Special dialog box, choose which format the Clipboard's data should be in when pasted into your document. You can do this by selecting the data format you want from the <u>A</u>s box. You can also click the Paste <u>L</u>ink radio button to make the Clipboard contents a *linked* object when pasted into your work.

Another way to paste the contents of the Clipboard is to click the <u>D</u>isplay As Icon option. When selected, this option shows the pasted object as a graphic icon. This can be handy if you want the object available for editing later but don't want to crowd or clutter your document's space with the entire pasted Clipboard.

Extra info

 Anything from the Clipboard that is pasted with the Edit⇨Paste Special command can be double-clicked in the document to open the object's original application that created it. This allows you to edit the file that the icon represents.

 You must Edit⇨Copy or Edit⇨Cut something in order to put its contents in the Windows Clipboard.

 Using the Edit⇨Paste Special command can make your computer creep, and in some cases, crash! Make sure that your computer has at least 8MB of system RAM before trying this special command out.

 Study the Insert⇨Object, Edit⇨Links, and Edit⇨Object commands in order to use the Edit⇨Paste Special command to its fullest.

Edit⇨Paste Text

This communications program command works the same way as the Edit⇨Paste command in other applications, except that it can only paste text data from the Windows Clipboard to your communication's window — not to charts, graphics, or forms.

Minimum mouse motion

Hot key hysteria

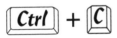

 This command is only found in the Works Communications accessory because only text data and text information are used and displayed in a communications session with another computer.

This command opens the Replace dialog box to help you search for text in your document and replace it with any other text that you choose.

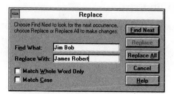

Ample info

1. Enter the text you want to find in the Find What box.

2. If you want to look for and replace only a whole word, click Match Whole Word Only to select that option. This option keeps the text you're searching for from showing up inside other words. For example, if you're looking for the word "rat," the Replace command skips over words such as "inspiration," "separation," and "rattle."

3. If the text that you want to replace has uppercase letters — like "Therefore" or "When" — you can click Match Case and you only find these words at the beginning of a sentence (or wherever else they happen to be capitalized).

4. Enter the text that you want for the replacement text in the Replace With box.

5. Click the Find Next button to start the search. The first occurrence of the word to be replaced is highlighted in your document.

6. Click the Replace button to replace the highlighted word in your document with the replacement word. If you don't want a word replaced, just click the Find Next button to skip over it and move to the next one.

   When you replace a word with the Replace button, click the Find Next button to continue your search.

7. If you want to replace all occurrences of a highlighted word in your document, click the Replace All button.

8. Works lets you know that you've reached the end of the document with an information box.

9. Click the Cancel button in the Replace dialog box or press Esc to quit the Edit⇨Replace command at any time.

Extra info

If you want to find certain text in your document and type in new text at each highlighted occurrence, then see the Edit⇨Find command.

Save your work (Ctrl+S) before using this command. Clicking the Replace All button in the dialog box can turn your document into a big mess if you're not careful.

Edit⇨Select All

This command selects everything in the current document, spreadsheet, database list, or database report.

Extra info

If you make a big mistake with this command, such as deleting your whole document or spreadsheet, don't forget the handy Ctrl+Z undo shortcut.

Edit⇨Select Column

This command is found in the Works spreadsheet program, and it selects the entire column of the highlighted cell.

Edit⇨Select Field

This command selects the entire field column from your cursor's location in the Works database list view.

Edit⇨Select Record

This command selects the entire record row of the selected cell in the Works database list view.

Edit⇨Select Row

This command selects the entire row of the highlighted cell in the Works spreadsheet.

Edit⇨Select Title Text

This command selects just the title text of the current chart in the Works spreadsheet charting program.

Edit⇨Series

This command opens the Series dialog box to allow editing of the cell references for the *series* of a chart.

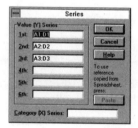

Ample info

The easiest way to use this command is to Edit⇨Cut or Edit⇨Copy the spreadsheet's cells that you want to reference in a chart. Then select your chart (View⇨Chart) and choose Series from the Edit menu. Click the series number you want changed from the Series dialog box. Finally, click the Paste button and then click OK or press Enter to insert the Clipboard's spreadsheet series as references for the chart to use.

Edit⇨Titles

This command opens the Titles dialog box, where you can enter the titles for various areas of the selected chart. Click OK to apply the new titles to the chart.

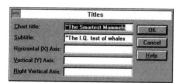

Edit⇨Undo

This command undoes your last command.

Hot key hysteria

$$Ctrl + Z$$

Extra info

The Edit⇨Undo command does not undo any mouse movement or keyboard keystroke.

File⇨Close

This command closes only the current word processing document, spreadsheet, chart, or database file — not the whole Works program.

Extra info

You can accomplish the same task by double clicking the document window's *control box* icon. This is the small square box that looks like the front of a file cabinet and is located in the upper-left corner of your document's window — not the one in the program's window.

Save your files before closing them. If you forget, a reminder dialog box appears asking if you want to save all the changes to the document before Works closes it.

Exiting Works using File⇨Exit Works shuts down the whole Works program. Use the File⇨Close command to close the active document only.

File⇨Create New File

This command opens the Startup dialog box so that you can choose the type of new file you want to create.

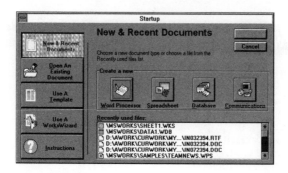

Ample info

In the Create A New section of the Startup dialog box, you can click one of the program buttons to create a new file type of your choosing. Click the Word Processor button to start a new Works word processor document, the Spreadsheet button to start a new Works spreadsheet document, the Database button to start a new Works database document, and the Communications button to open the Works modem program for starting a new communications session.

At the bottom of the dialog box, you can open Recently used files. Find a file that already exists from this list and double-click the file's name to open it.

You can create as many databases, spreadsheets, and word documents as you want — all the documents that you open become the contents of the Works *Workspace. Default* filenames for all the workspace documents are used by Works until the new files are saved using your own filenames.

Extra info

You've probably seen this Startup dialog box before. It's used with the following commands: File⇨Templates, File⇨Open Existing File, and File⇨WorksWizards. When these commands open the Startup dialog box, the appropriate function button in the left button column is selected (appears depressed) already.

If you save each individual Works file that is currently open and then save the Works workspace (File⇨Save Workspace), then all of the current document files will automatically open when you open the Works program again.

See File⇨Save Workspace.

File⇨Exit Works

If you want to shut'er down fast, use this command.

Ample info

When you choose this command, all of Microsoft Works for Windows closes. If there are any open documents left open that were not saved, Works opens a dialog box asking if you want to save these files before losing them forever.

Extra info

You can accomplish the same task by double clicking the Works *control box* icon. This is the small square box that looks like the front of a file cabinet to the left of the Works title bar.

Remember to save your Works files before exiting. If you forget, a reminder dialog box appears asking if you want to do so.

Exiting Works using File⇨Exit Works shuts down the whole Works program, but using File⇨Close closes only the active Works document.

File⇨Open Existing File

This command displays the Open dialog box to help you find and open your Works files from a disk.

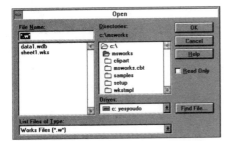

Ample info

If you see the filename in the File Name list box, double-click it to open it, but if your filename doesn't appear in the File Name list box, then click the down arrow to the right of the List Files of Type box and select Works Files (*.w*) from the drop down list. If you still don't see your file in the File Name list, select the correct drive from the Drives list and the directory from the Directories list where your Works files were saved. Highlight the file that you want and then click the OK button to open the file for Works and close the Open dialog box.

You may want to experiment with the File Organizer Works-Wizard by clicking the Find File button in the Open dialog box. This WorksWizard dialog box lists any type of file on any drive from the options you choose in this dialog box.

Extra info

See Chapter 2 in *Microsoft Works 3 For Windows For Dummies* for more information about using the File Organizer WorksWizard.

The *DOS For Dummies* or *Windows For Dummies* books can show you how to create new directories on your drive. Keeping files in your own file directory system helps you to organize them so you can find older files more easily.

File ⇨ Page Setup

This command opens the Page Setup dialog box where you can select from many page options that affect how your work appears on a printed page.

Ample info

Click at the top of the dialog box to select a *tab*. The Page Setup dialog box is divided into three tab options.

The Margins tab shows the changeable settings for the Top, Bottom, Left, and Right page margin, including extra space at the top of the page for your Header margin and some space at the bottom of the page for your Footer margin. Click the Reset button to start over with the margin's default settings, or just click Cancel to quit the dialog box.

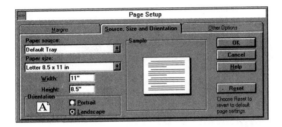

The paper choices that the Source, Size, and Orientation tab of the Page Setup dialog box offers are the Paper source (tells your printer which stack of paper to print on), the standard Paper size choices, and the Width and Height of any custom page dimensions you may need. To choose how the document is placed on the paper, click either the Portrait or the Landscape Orientation radio button. Check the sample from time to time for a thumbnail view of how the page looks. If you really mess things up, click the Reset button in the dialog box to start over or click the Cancel button to close the Page Setup dialog box.

The Other Options tab allows you to specify your starting page number on the current document in the 1st page number box. You may want to Print footnotes at the end of the document, too. Click the Reset button to start over with the tab's default settings, or just click Cancel to quit the dialog box.

Extra info

Clicking the Cancel button in any one of the three dialog box tabs cancels out any changes to the options made to the other two tabs, too.

See File⇨Print or File⇨Print Preview for other ways to change the overall size, style, and design of your document's printed page.

File⇨Print

This command opens the Print dialog box for choosing how the Works documents look when you print them.

Minimum mouse motion

Hot key hysteria

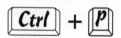

Ample info

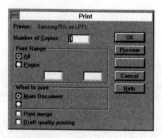

The type of options in the Print dialog box varies with the make and model of the printer that is connected to your computer. For the most part, the Number of Copies, the Print Range, What to print, and Draft quality printing are standard Print dialog box options. If you want to see the full page on the screen before you print it on paper, click the Preview button. From the print preview view, you can zoom in, turn pages, Print, or just click Cancel if the preview doesn't look right. If you click the Cancel button, the settings in the Print dialog box will be retained. The print preview in the File⇨Print command is the same one accessed through the Print Preview button on the toolbar or the one used by the File⇨Print Preview command.

Extra info

 You might need to look up your printer's special printing options in its operation manual. The extra info will help you print the pages exactly the way you want them to look.

 See File⇨Page Setup and File⇨Print Preview for other ways to change the overall size, style, and design of your document's printed page.

 Don't forget to load paper in the printer and turn the power on. Also, check your manual to see if the on-line mode must be switched on manually — if so, do that too before clicking the OK button to start printing.

File⇨Print Preview

This command switches you from the current display window into the Print Preview window, which shows you how the document will look when it's printed on paper.

Minimum mouse motion

Ample info

By clicking on different buttons in the Print Preview window, you can do the following: Zoom In or Zoom Out, turn to the Next page or back to the Previous page, Print, or just click Cancel to quit the whole print job. This print preview window is the same one you see when you click the Preview button in the Print dialog box (File⇨Print).

Extra info

 See File⇨Print and File⇨Page Setup for other ways to change the overall size, style, and design of your document's page.

TIP
When you Zoom In on the Print Preview window, use the horizontal and vertical scroll bars to view close-up portions of the document's page.

File⇨Printer Setup

Before printing, choose the printer that you want to use and its options from this command's Printer Setup dialog box.

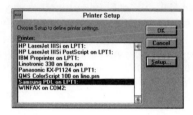

Ample info

The type of options in the Printer Setup dialog box varies with the make and model of the printer that is connected to your computer. Click on the printer name from the Printer list and then click OK to save your choices and close the dialog box.

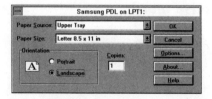

After you choose a printer, click the Setup button to set up other aspects of your printer from yet another dialog box.

Extra info

See File⇨Print and File⇨Page Setup for other ways to change the overall size, style, and design of your document's printed page.

File⇨Save

This command saves your current document to a file on a disk.

Minimum mouse motion

Hot key hysteria

$\boxed{Ctrl}$ + $\boxed{S}$

Ample info

If you choose the Save command from the File menu or click the Save button in the toolbar, the current file and all the changes are saved to your disk. If your file is new and has never been saved, you are given the Save As dialog box.

Extra info

See the File⇨Save As command if you receive the Save As dialog box when saving a particular document for the first time.

File⇨Save As

This command opens the Save As dialog box, where you can choose how you want to save a new document that has not yet been saved to a disk. You can also save the current document with a different name or in a different type of file format by using this command. Works always places the proper *filename extension* with its period on the filenames for you.

Ample info

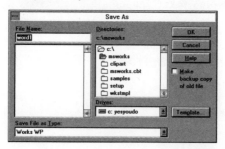

Type a filename for your document in the File Name list box. Click the down arrow to the right of the List Files of Type box to save the document in a different file format — this can be handy if someone needs to use your file but does not have the Works program. Choose which drive you want to send the file to from the Drives list, and then choose which directory you want to save the file in from the Directories list. Click the OK button or press Enter to save the file to your disk and close the Save As dialog box.

Extra info

The *DOS For Dummies* or *Windows For Dummies* books can help you to learn how to organize and save files in your own file directory system.

If you click the Templates button in the Save As dialog box, you are greeted with the Save As Template dialog box. If you want to save your file as a template, you must first type a name for your template in the Template Name text box and click the OK button or just press Enter. The template's new name becomes a template name in the Choose a template list box of the Startup dialog box. Next you see the Save As dialog box. This is the same dialog box used by the File⇨Save As command. Refer to the preceding paragraphs to complete these steps.

Check out the File⇨Templates command to see why you might want to save the current document as a template file.

See Chapter 4 in *Microsoft Works 3 For Windows For Dummies* for more information about how to save Works files so that they can be used by other Windows and DOS programs.

File⇨Save Workspace

This command saves the current layout of Works *workspace*.

Ample info

If you want all of the Works documents that you currently have open to open each time you open Works, then here's what to do. First, save every Works file that is open. Then save the Works workspace (File⇨Save Workspace) so that all the of the Works document files open automatically when the Works program is opened later. If you forget to save each document in the workspace first, Works alerts you with an information box. When you open Works later, all the Works document's windows have the same size and position.

Extra info

Use this command when you know you will be working on the same set of Works files later — it's a real time-saver.

File⇨Send

Using this command, you can send files to anyone who is connected to your computer network.

Ample info

Since networks connecting computers are as different as fingerprints on people, ask your friendly network guru how to use this command.

Extra info

If the Send command from the File menu is grayed out — making it unusable — then your computer is not connected to a network system. If a network is added later, reload the Works program — this makes the File⇨Send command usable.

File⇨Templates

This command opens the Startup dialog box where you can choose a Works predesigned template and open it from a list of *template* groups, categories, and names.

Ample info

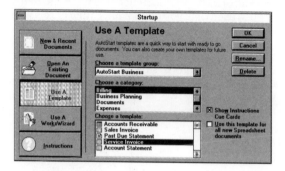

Choose a template group that is appropriate first and then Choose a category that fits your needs. Finally, Choose a template that you want to use from the list and click the OK button or just press Enter. The Startup dialog box closes and the template is opened in the Works program.

If you think the template you choose is the cat's pajamas, click the Use this template for all new check box to select it. This option sends the chosen template to either a new Works spreadsheet, database, or word processor document to use whenever a new file is created by Works using the File⇨Create New File command. If you want to open a new file occasionally that does not use this template, then you'll have to uncheck this option later.

If you click the Show Instructions Cue Cards option's box before opening a template, you are greeted with numerous instructions from the Cue Cards dialog box while working in the template. If you get tired of Cue Cards' verbose interruptions, click the Close button in the Cue Cards dialog box to turn them off.

Extra info

The Startup dialog box that is opened with the File⇨Templates command is the same dialog box used by the File⇨Create New File command, the File⇨Open Existing File command, and the File⇨WorksWizards command. When these commands open the Startup dialog box, the appropriate function button that matches the command is already selected (appears depressed) in the left button column.

You can use templates in about the same way you use WorksWizards — but templates ask fewer questions.

See the File⇨WorksWizards command. It's a similar type of helping command.

File⇨Works Wizards

This command opens the WorksWizards dialog box so that you can choose a ready-made document.

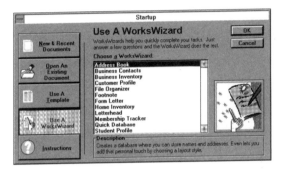

Ample info

You can choose a WorksWizard from the Choose a WorksWizard list. A description of the highlighted document's usefulness is displayed in the Description area of the Startup dialog box. When you find the right WorksWizard for the job ahead, click OK. If you answer the WorksWizard's questions and follow its directions from the dialog box prompts that follow, you can create your own tailored document.

This WorksWizard can save lots of precious time — especially when you are just learning the Works program.

Extra info

Use WorksWizard to open a document and practice with it. Tear it apart. Investigate its graphics. Search its spreadsheet cells and database forms. As in medicine, dissection is a precious, hands-on learning experience.

The Startup dialog box that is opened with the File⇨WorksWizard command is the same dialog box used by the File⇨Create New File command, the File⇨Open Existing File command, and the File⇨Templates command. When these commands open the Startup dialog box, the appropriate command-matching button is selected (appears depressed) in the left button column of the dialog box.

Format⇨Add Border

Add a border around the current chart from the spreadsheet charting program with this command.

Ample info

All the chart borders created using the Format⇨Add Border command are the same distance from the chart, and there are no options to change the line thickness or color.

Extra info

If you want to create your own colorful border around a chart, go to a word processor document and use the Insert⇨Drawing command to create a new border using Microsoft Draw. A chart can then be cut (or copied) and pasted on top of the custom border.

To add other types of borders in other types of Works documents, check out the Format⇨Border command.

Too many borders around charts, clip art, and other graphics can make a document hard to read. Be careful in your use of borders.

Format⇨Add Legend

This command displays a *legend* in your chart.

Ample info

The legends of a chart are the shaded, patterned, or colored labeled boxes that show what the bars, lines, and pie segments represent — just like legends on a road map or atlas. When the Add Legend command is active, a check mark is displayed next to it in the Format menu. If the command is not active, there is no check mark by it. Choosing the Format⇨Add Legend command repeatedly turns your chart's legend on and off.

Format⇨Alignment

You can use this command to set the *alignment* of the text in a spreadsheet's cell. The Format⇨Alignment command is also available to align the text in a database form, or to align data in the cells of a database list.

Minimum mouse motion

These toolbar buttons are a quick way to align text in the cells of a spreadsheet. In a database list or form, you must use the Format⇨Alignment command's dialog box because no alignment buttons are available on the database toolbar.

Ample info

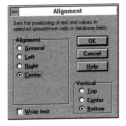

When working with highlighted cells in a database list, click one of the Alignment options in the Alignment dialog box to choose your horizontal text position. Then click either the Top, Center, or Bottom for the text's Vertical position. One click on the Wrap text option sizes the cell so that any long text shows instead of disappearing beyond the left and right borders of the cell. Click OK or press Enter to apply all the text positioning options to the highlighted cells of the database list.

While a database is in the form view, the Alignment dialog box has the Slide to left option added to it. Click on the Slide to left option box to get rid of any extra blank white space that can show up between two fields on a printed form.

In the Alignment dialog box of a spreadsheet, two extra options are added. The Fill option makes your highlighted cells duplicate the text, value, or formula that is in the selected cells. The Center across selection option makes any text in a highlighted row of cells centered within the group of selected cells.

Extra info

The height of a Wrap text cell must be raised so that all of its text can be displayed.

See the Format⇨Row Height command to change the height of a spreadsheet's cell.

The Format⇨Alignment command only aligns cell text, not paragraph text.

Format⇨AutoFormat

This handy little command gives your current spreadsheet table a professional, finished look.

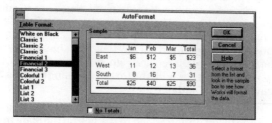

Ample info

Click the name of the format that you want from the Table Format
list. This list is long, so click the vertical *scroll bar* to scroll
through the list. The Sample area of the dialog box shows you a
thumbnail of the format you choose from this list. If you don't
want any totals to show in your table, click the No Totals box to
select it. Click the OK button or press Enter to apply the chosen
format to the highlighted cells of your spreadsheet.

Extra info

Use the Format⇨AutoFormat command when you want to leave
work early.

Don't let the boss catch you leaving work early.

Format⇨Border

This command lets you use the options in the Border dialog box
to create custom borders in a word document, spreadsheet,
database list, database form, or database report.

Ample info

One of three slightly different Border dialog boxes can open,
depending on which type of document you're currently using.
Choose a listed Line Style and then a Color from the drop-down
list. You may choose to add a border to the cell or box by
selecting from the Border list. Press Enter to apply your options
to the cell or box, or press Esc to quit the dialog box without
applying the options.

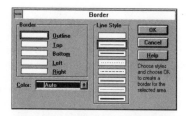

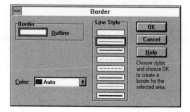

 ## Extra info

See the Format⇨Add Border command to add a border around a spreadsheet's chart.

Too many borders around the charts, clip art, and other graphics in a document can make it hard to read. Be careful not to use too many borders.

Format⇨Bring To Front

This command brings a selected object to the front of all other objects in a database form.

 ## Extra info

An item in Works must be selected or highlighted first so that this command is available.

Format⇨Column Width

This command sets the width of the columns in a database report or spreadsheet. Type the number of the characters that you want to fit across the column's width in the Width box of the Column Width dialog box.

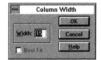

Extra info

The Format⇨Columns command gives you options for setting up text columns on a page in a word processor document.

You can *drag* the left or right border of a column by pointing the mouse cursor just above a column's boundary in the label heading area of your spreadsheet or database list. Drag the border to adjust the width of a column when you see the mouse cursor change to a double-arrowhead cursor that is labeled ADJUST.

Chapter 15 in *Microsoft Works 3 For Windows For Dummies* explains more about adjusting the size of a table's rows and columns using the mouse.

Format⇨Columns

This command's dialog box offers choices for creating custom text columns on a page in a word processor document.

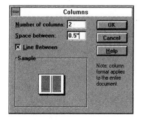

Ample info

To set up your column page, enter the Number of columns and the Space between the columns in inches. If you want a Line Between the columns, click its box to select it. The display in the Sample area of the dialog box shows you a preview of the column page. Click OK to apply the dialog box entries to the column page or click Cancel to quit the command and close the dialog box.

Extra info

To see the columns in your document, switch to the page layout view by choosing Page Layout from the View menu in the word processor.

The Format⇨Column Width command handles the column options for a database report or spreadsheet only — not a word processor document.

Format⇨Field Size

This command brings up the Field Size dialog box, where you can set up the overall size for the selected data entry line in a database form.

Ample info

The Field Size dialog box displays the selected field's Name, along with a Width text box and a Height text box for entering your own field sizes. The value used in the Width text box represents the number of text characters and/or spaces, while the Height value is the number of text lines.

Extra info

See the Format⇨Field Width command to learn how to set up the column widths in a database list.

Format⇨Field Width

This command sets the (column) width of a field in a database list.

Ample info

You can enter the number of text characters and/or spaces for the field in the Width text box or click the Best Fit option to tell Works to adjust the field's width to accommodate the longest string of text in a field's column in a database list.

Extra info

See the Format⇨Record Height command to control the height of each record (row) in a database list.

Clicking the Best Fit option in the Field Width dialog box is the best way to ensure that all entered data in the field's column is visible — no matter how much you type into it.

Format⇨Font and Style

The dialog box for this command controls all the characteristics of the selected (highlighted) text in any Works document.

Minimum mouse motion

These font formatting buttons are found in the toolbar of the Works word processor, spreadsheet, and database.

Hot key hysteria

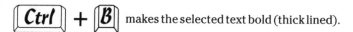

Ctrl + **B** makes the selected text bold (thick lined).

Ctrl + **I** makes the selected text italic (slanted).

Ctrl + **U** makes the selected text underlined.

Ample info

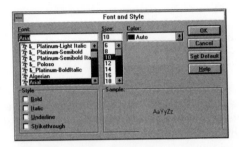

The Font and Style dialog box offers you an added selection of Color for the highlighted text in your document. Click the down arrow in the Color box to choose a color other than the black default. The other Font and Style dialog box selections can be accessed quickly by clicking a style or font button in the toolbar or by pressing the correct hot key combination. If you would rather use the dialog box, then scroll through the Font and Size boxes to choose the option you need. In the Style section, click the styles you want for your highlighted text. If you change your mind about your selections, just click the Set Default button to set your dialog box color choices as the default ones. When you're satisfied with what you see in the Sample area, click OK or press Enter to close the dialog box and apply the changes to your text.

Extra info

Memorizing the style hot key combinations instead of using the Format⇨Font and Style command saves you lots of time.

The only reason you need to use the Format⇨Font and Style command is to change the color of your selected text.

Read all about adding fonts to Windows in *Windows For Dummies*. Any new fonts that you add to Windows become available in the Font and Style dialog box of Works the next time you use it.

Format⇨Freeze Titles

This command freezes the titles in the current spreadsheet.

Ample info

If you use this command to freeze the titles you preselect in a spreadsheet, you can search through a large spreadsheet using the *scroll bars* while keeping the frozen titles in view at all times during your sheet search.

Extra info

Another way to accomplish the same results as the Format⇨Freeze Titles command is to use the Split command from the Window menu.

See the Window⇨Split command for more information about how to control the windows in the Works spreadsheet, database, or word processor.

Format⇨Horizontal (X) Axis

This command opens the Horizontal Axis dialog box for controlling the X axis scaling options in any current chart (except a pie chart).

Ample info

When working with a bar or area chart, the Horizontal Axis dialog box gives you four choices. Click the first one, Show Gridlines, when you need to see a vertical grid in a complex chart. The gridlines identify the different sets of series (the bars) more easily. When working with an area chart with the Show Droplines option selected, vertical lines are drawn between each point on the X axis and the chart's plotted line. If you don't want tic marks to show up on the horizontal axis of your chart, click the No Horizontal Axis box. Finally, double-clicking the text box at the bottom of the dialog box lets you type in a new custom Label frequency rate. The frequency rate determines how often labels are displayed on the X axis. A common rate used for the frequency of chart labels is twelve — for dividing the month's values with the only the years labeled.

When working with a line or scatter chart, a different Horizontal Axis dialog box opens for setting the <u>M</u>inimum, Ma<u>x</u>imum, and the <u>I</u>nterval of its horizontal values. Clicking the Show <u>G</u>ridlines option gives you vertical, dashed lines in your chart so that you can read it more easily. When you select the Use <u>L</u>ogarithmic Scale option, the horizontal axis changes from a numerical scale to a logarithmic one. The Use <u>L</u>ogarithmic Scale option is usually chosen when you're working with very large X values or high value intervals.

Extra info

Experiment with the horizontal axis of your chart to see how the settings in the Horizontal Axis dialog box change it.

To control options for the Y axis, see the Forma<u>t</u>⇨<u>V</u>ertical (Y) Axis command.

Format⇨Make 3-D

This command changes the current two-dimensional chart into a 3-D chart.

Minimum mouse motion

These 3-D charting toolbar buttons not only change the style of your current chart, but they also make it a 3-D chart. The Forma<u>t</u>⇨Make <u>3</u>-D command can only change the current chart's style into a 3-D type chart with the same style. In other words, if you have a pie chart as the current chart and choose the Forma<u>t</u>⇨Make <u>3</u>-D command—the resulting chart is still a pie, but it is now in 3-D, but if you click the Display a 3-D Line Chart button instead, the style changes to a 3-D chart with a line style too.

Extra info

You can see other types of charts by choosing any one of the first twelve commands from the <u>G</u>allery menu in the Works spread-sheet charting program. They are in order as follows: <u>G</u>allery⇨<u>A</u>rea, <u>G</u>allery⇨<u>B</u>ar, <u>G</u>allery⇨<u>L</u>ine, <u>G</u>allery⇨<u>P</u>ie,

Gallery⇨Stacked Line, Gallery⇨X-Y (Scatter), Gallery⇨Radar, Gallery⇨Combination, Gallery⇨3-D Area, Gallery⇨3-D Bar, Gallery⇨3-D Line, and Gallery⇨3-D Pie.

Format⇨Mixed Line and Bar

In the Mixed Line and Bar dialog box, click the radio buttons (Line A, Line B, Line C...) of the Y series that you want to display as a line chart. You can emphasize the results of a particular series in your current bar chart by using this command. The added lines in a bar chart emphasize the length differences of the bars.

Format⇨Number

This command formats the numbers in the cells of a spreadsheet or database list. It also formats the *fields* in a database form or report. If you format the cells or field areas before you enter any data, the data changes automatically to the new format as you type it into the cell or field.

Minimum mouse motion

The currency formatting button is available in the spreadsheet toolbar. Select a cell or cell block and then click the currency button to change all the selected cells to a currency format.

Ample info

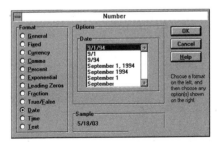

Choose a data entry format by clicking one of its radio buttons in the Format list. The options for the selected format are listed in the Options box. Scroll through the Options box to find the format option you want and click it to highlight it. To check how your format option looks in your document, read the sample in the Sample section at the bottom of the dialog box. Click OK to apply your choice to the selection in your document.

Extra info

Before using the Format⇨Number command, you must first select some cells in a database list or spreadsheet, or you must select a field in a database report or form.

Using the Format⇨Number command makes entering data in the Works program much faster and easier. It also helps you to keep the data format more consistent throughout your documents.

To see what the format options for the Format⇨Number command represent, check out Parts III and IV of *Microsoft Works 3 For Windows For Dummies*.

Format⇨Paragraph

This command opens the Paragraph dialog box in a word document. Choose which options to display in the Paragraph dialog box by clicking on the Quick Formats tab, the Indents and Alignment tab, or the Breaks and Spacing tab.

Minimum mouse motion

Clicking one of the following three toolbar buttons changes the alignment of the current paragraph.

Clicking this toolbar button changes the current paragraph to and from a bulleted one.

Hot key hysteria

⎢Ctrl⎢ + ⎢L⎢

Pressing Ctrl+L aligns the paragraph to the left margin.

⎢Ctrl⎢ + ⎢E⎢

Pressing Ctrl+E aligns the paragraph to the center margin.

⎢Ctrl⎢ + ⎢R⎢

Pressing Ctrl+R aligns the paragraph to the right margin.

Ample info

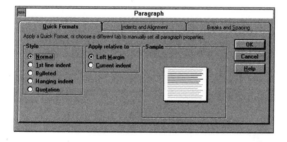

The Quick Formats tab of the Paragraph dialog box gives you
options for the style of the current paragraph and shows you how
to apply them. Choose a style from the Style list by clicking its
radio button. Notice that the Sample box shows what the paragraph looks like when a style is chosen. You can apply the chosen
style to the current paragraph relative to the text being in the Left
Margin (this option removes any current paragraph indenting
when applying the new style), or choose the Current indent
option to apply a style to a paragraph that is already indented
(this option keeps any current paragraph's initial indentation
when applying the new style).

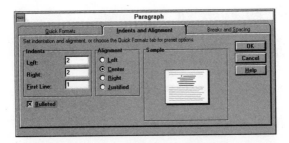

From the Indents and Alignment tab of the Paragraph dialog box,
you can customize the way the current paragraph is placed on
the page. In the Indents section, choose how large you want the
Left and Right indents to be and which indent you want to give to
the First Line of the current paragraph. Click a radio button from
the Alignment section of the dialog box to tell Works how you
want the paragraph aligned between the page's margins. Don't
forget about the little check box option in the lower-left corner of
the dialog box — click it to turn the current paragraph into a
Bulleted one.

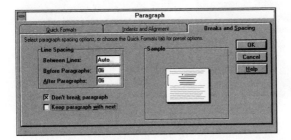

The Breaks and Spacing tab of the Paragraph dialog box lets you
determine the line spacing of a paragraph and also how you want
Works to treat the current paragraph when it is too large to fit on
one page and must print on two pages.

Let's say you want to type a paragraph that contains a list, and
you want to follow that list with a descriptive paragraph. To do
so, you can select the paragraph that contains the list and

- Set your Between Lines spacing to single-space by typing
  1li in the text box. Your list paragraph becomes single
  spaced.

- Set your line spacing Before Paragraphs to a double space
  by typing **2li** in the text box — this separates your list from
  the preceding paragraph.

- Set your line spacing After Paragraphs to a triple space by typing **3li** in the text box. This puts a triple space between the list and the descriptive paragraph that follows it.

- When you click the Don't break paragraph option, the list does not get sent to another page if only half of it fits on a page. In other words, clicking this option keeps your paragraph from splitting between the bottom of one page and the top of the next.

- The Keep paragraph with next option must be selected to make the list paragraph and descriptive paragraph stay together on the same page.

Extra info

Use the toolbar buttons often and memorize the hot key combos to bypass the lengthy Paragraph dialog box.

All of the formatting options chosen in the Paragraph dialog box are applied to the current paragraph (the one with the blinking cursor in it) when you click the dialog box's OK button.

To change the format of a new paragraph, press Enter to create the new paragraph. Then choose the paragraph options using the Format⇨Paragraph command, click OK to close the Paragraph dialog box, and start typing the paragraph. The text that you type matches the format chosen in the Paragraph dialog box.

Format⇨Patterns

This command fills the current column in a database list, the selected data entry box in a database form, or the selected fields of a database report with a color pattern chosen from the Patterns dialog box.

Minimum mouse motion

Clicking the Learning Works button on the toolbar and then clicking the Use a WorksWizard button that appears creates new documents with the help of the WorksWizard dialog box. The process is so easy and is great for beginners.

Just follow the simple directions in each dialog box and answer a few questions and pick from some options to create a new Works document. If you decide to quit using the WorksWizard, click the Cancel button at any time.

Ample info

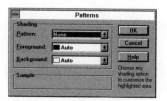

You can choose a **P**attern, a **F**oreground color, and a **B**ackground color by clicking on the down arrow from the appropriate drop-down list in the Patterns dialog box. You may want to proof the design of your pattern in the Sample area at the bottom of the dialog box before applying the pattern to your selection.

Extra info

To make changes to patterns in a chart, you must use the Format⇨Patterns and Colors command.

Format⇨Patterns and Colors

This chart command allows you to change the patterns and colors of the different Y *series* of a chart. It also offers you the color and pattern choices for a pie slice when working with a pie chart.

Minimum mouse motion

Clicking the Learning Works button on the toolbar (the one with a question mark in it) and then clicking the Use a WorksWizard button gives you a selection of charts that were color coordinated by the Microsoft crew. (I didn't say they were good designers!)

Ample info

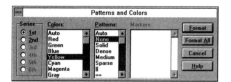

To change the fill of a Y series, click the radio button of the Series that you want to change. Then choose a color from the scroll box's list of C<u>o</u>lors. Select a pattern from the <u>P</u>atterns scroll box that uses your color choices and then click the <u>F</u>ormat button to apply your choice to the selected series. If you want to apply the colored pattern choices to all of the series in the chart, click the Format <u>A</u>ll button — but don't ask me why you would want to do that.

The same steps apply when you are working with a pie chart, except that the Series section of the Patterns and Colors dialog box is called <u>S</u>lices. You also get an extra dialog box option when working with pie charts. If the <u>E</u>xplode Slice option is selected when you click the <u>F</u>ormat button, Works takes the selected pie slice chosen from the <u>S</u>lices section and pulls it away from the rest of the pie in the chart for emphasis. Mmmm! I'm hungry already.

Extra info

When the <u>E</u>xplode Slice option is selected, don't click the Format <u>A</u>ll button in the Patterns and Colors dialog box — this makes the pie chart look like last year's Thanksgiving leftovers.

When you work with any chart, you can customize it with the commands from the Forma<u>t</u> menu.

To change a chart, you must first make one. Check out the T<u>o</u>ols ⇨ <u>C</u>reate New Chart command to create a chart from your spreadsheet.

Format ⇨ Picture/Object

You can change the <u>S</u>ize of a selected picture graphic or object with this command found in the word processor or database form. A <u>T</u>ext Wrap tab is available in the Picture/Object dialog box of the word processor. This tab gives you options that control how text flows around the graphics on your document page.

Minimum mouse motion

When you select a graphic, eight small handles appear around its perimeter. Click and drag these handles with your mouse to size the graphic.

Ample info

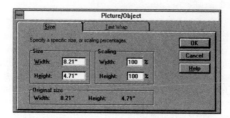

You can change the Width and Height sizes of the graphic by entering new sizes in the Size section's text boxes, or you can change the Width and Height scaling by entering new scale percentages in the Scaling section's text boxes. At the bottom of the dialog box, the Original size of the graphic is displayed so you won't forget what you started with before changing the graphic.

When using the Format⇨Picture/Object command in the word processor, you can click the Text Wrap tab at the top of the Picture/Object dialog box to determine the way the document's text surrounds the selected graphic and what distance the text is positioned from the graphic.

Extra info

When working with a database form, the Format⇨Picture/Object command is not available (not even listed) until a picture or object is inserted on the database form.

Format⇨Protection

This command offers ways to protect your data in a spreadsheet or a database and to keep it from being accidentally changed or deleted.

Ample info

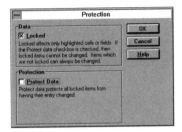

To lock the cells of a spreadsheet or the fields of a database list to keep them from getting moved, click on the Locked option check box in the Protection dialog box. To keep spreadsheet cells or database fields from getting changed or deleted, click the Protect Data check box. While working in a database form, click the Protect Form option to keep from accidentally changing the form.

Extra info

If you protect some data or forms with this command, don't forget to use this same command to turn off the protection when you want to edit the data or change some aspects of the form.

Format⇨Record Height

This command sets the height of a *record* in a database list.

Ample info

If you need taller cells in a database list to fit a large font size, enter the height (in point size) that you want for the selected records in the Height text box. Click Best Fit to let Works do its own thing with the record's height. Click OK or press Enter to keep the new height choice and close the dialog box.

Extra info

If you don't want some records (rows of cells) to be seen on your computer monitor while you are working with a database list, select them and then use the Format⇨Record Height command and give the rows a height of one point — which hides the rows.

If you select a field (column) in a database list and apply the Format⇨Record Height command, all the records (rows) change in height.

Format⇨Right Vertical (Y) Axis

This command controls the scaling of the right side axis on a double-vertical (Y) axis chart.

This command controls the right vertical (Y) axis in the same manner the Format⇨Vertical (Y) Axis command controls the left vertical (Y) axis — even their dialog boxes are identical. Refer to the Format⇨Vertical (Y) Axis command for details.

Extra info

This command is only available when the current chart has a left and right Y axis. To create a double vertical (Y) axis chart, use the Format⇨Two Vertical (Y) Axis command.

Format⇨Row Height

This command sets the height of a row in a spreadsheet or a database report.

Ample info

In the Row Height dialog box, enter the new height (point size) for the selected rows of the spreadsheet or database report in the Height text box. Click the Best Fit box to let Works do its own thing with the rows' height. Click OK or press Enter to close the dialog box and apply the new height to your rows.

Extra info

If you don't want any of the data in your spreadsheet to be seen, select everything with the Edit⇨Select All command and then use the Format⇨Row Height command to give the selected rows a height of one point. (This height setting makes the rows too small to show the data that is in them.)

To set the width of a column in a spreadsheet or database report, use the Format⇨Column Width command.

Format⇨Send To Back

This command sends the selected object to the back of all other objects on a database form.

Extra info

You cannot choose this command from the menu unless you have selected or highlighted something first.

Format⇨Set Print Area

This command allows you to mark a selected part of the spreadsheet and print only the marked portion.

Ample info

Highlight the part of the spreadsheet that you want to print. Choose the Set Print Area command from the Format menu and click OK in the confirmation dialog box that follows. You can now print this selected area of your spreadsheet. Clicking anywhere else in the spreadsheet deselects the print area.

Extra info

After you select the print area and use the Format⇨Set Print Area command, be careful not to accidentally deselect the print area by clicking someplace else in your spreadsheet. Doing so deselects the print area and causes the entire spreadsheet to print.

Format⇨Show Field Name

When selected in the Format menu, the Show Field Name command makes all the field names visible in a database form. When the command is deselected, the field names become invisible.

Format⇨Snap To Grid

This command, used in a database form, activates a grid to help you lay out forms.

Ample info

When the Snap to Grid command is preceded by a check mark in the Format menu, it is active. When no check mark appears next to the command, then the *snap to grid* feature is inactive. When active, the snap to grid acts as a magnet, and objects placed around the form become magically attracted to the intersection points in the grid layout. (Wow! What a music video concept!) This feature helps you to keep the pictures, objects, and text more organized by ensuring that everything in the database form is in line and evenly spaced.

Extra info

It's best to leave the snap to grid feature on at all times.

Format⇨Tabs

Use this command when you want to precisely set your document's tab positions, alignment, and leaders.

Minimum mouse motion

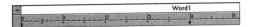

Drag the default tab marks (the upside-down Ts) on the ruler to adjust them to a new position. Click a new position in the ruler to add a new tab. Double-clicking anywhere on the ruler opens the Tabs dialog box. If the ruler is not visible, use the View⇨Ruler command to turn it on.

Ample info

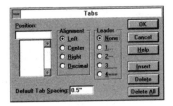

To add a custom tab to the document, type the tab's distance from the left margin in the Position text box and then click the Insert button to add the new tab's position to the Position list. Repeat this procedure to create more custom tabs. To delete a tab, select it from the Position list and click the Delete button. Clicking the Delete All button deletes every tab in your document.

All the new tabs you create are Left Alignment ones by default. If you want a new tab to be a Center, Right, or Decimal one instead, click the appropriate radio button in the Alignment section of the Tabs dialog box.

When you want a leader for your tab, click one of the radio buttons in the Leader section to select the style you want.

The default setting for tabs in a new word processor document is one tab spaced every 0.5˝ (one-half inch). If you need a tab every two inches, Type 2˝ in the Default Tab Spacing text box.

Extra info

Not only can you drag the tab marks in a ruler to reposition them, you can also drag the margin marks and the indent marks to new positions, too.

Most of the indenting in your word processor document is controlled by the formatting style of the paragraphs, not by the tab settings. See the Format⇨Paragraph command for a better way to indent and align text.

If you accidentally erase all your tabs with the Delete All button in the Tabs dialog box, just use the Undo command on the Edit menu to restore them to their original positions, or simply press Ctrl+Z.

Format⇨Two Vertical (Y) Axes

This command creates a second vertical (Y) axis on the right side of the current chart using the selected value series in the Two Vertical Axes dialog box.

Ample info

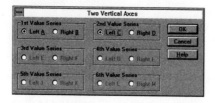

Click one or more of the Right radio buttons in the Value Series you want duplicated to the right vertical (Y) axis. Click the OK button to add the axis to the current chart.

Extra info

Select every Right radio button in every Value Series that is active in the Two Vertical Axes dialog box to create a duplicate of the left axis on the right side.

Use the Format⇨Right Vertical (Y) Axis command to change the scaling properties of the right vertical (Y) axis after creating two vertical axes for your chart.

 You can't use the Format⇨Two Vertical (Y) Axes command when working with a pie chart.

Format⇨Vertical (Y) Axis

This command opens a Vertical Axis dialog box for controlling the vertical (Y) axis scale options in any chart other than a pie chart.

Ample info

Changing the settings in the Vertical Axis dialog box controls the Y axis of a bar or area chart. Select Show Gridlines when you need a horizontal gridline to show. Doing this helps you to read a complex chart and to follow the values (the height in a bar chart) of the X series. When you select the Use Logarithmic Scale option, the vertical axis changes from a numerical scale to a logarithmic one. You should choose the Logarithmic option when you're working with very large Y values or high value intervals. If you don't want the tic marks to display on the vertical axis of the chart, click the No Vertical Axis option. If you want to customize the proportion of a chart's Y axis, type new ranges for the Y values in the Minimum, Maximum, and Interval text boxes.

Extra info

 Experiment with the settings in the Vertical Axis dialog box to see how the different settings change your chart.

 To control the scaling options for the X axis, see the Format⇨Horizontal (X) Axis command.

Gallery ⇨ 3-D Area

This command changes the current chart into a 3-D area chart of your choice.

Minimum mouse motion

Ample info

This type of chart is a fancy way of showing the changes and comparisons of several data series over a period of time, while emphasizing the amount of changes or similarities that occur in the data by showing the cumulative totals for each series. When using this command, the 3-D Area dialog box displays several samples of 3-D charts for you to choose from. To choose a new style for your chart, just double-click the one you want from the samples in the dialog box.

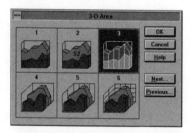

The following list describes each sample chart in the dialog box:

- Dialog box sample number one is a standard 3-D area chart.

- Dialog box sample number two is a 3-D area chart with *legend* text and *series* labels.

- Dialog box sample number three is a 3-D area chart with *droplines.*

- Dialog box sample number four is a 3-D area chart with separate series.

- Dialog box sample number five is a 3-D area chart with separate series and vertical *gridlines.*

- Dialog box sample number six is a 3-D area chart with separate series and both vertical and horizontal gridlines.

Extra info

Clicking the Next or Previous button in the 3-D Area dialog box shows samples of the different chart styles. You can accomplish the same task by choosing a different chart style command from the Gallery menu, but using the dialog box buttons is faster.

You must create a chart first by using the Tools⇨Create New Chart command in a spreadsheet before you can change a chart's style with a command from the Gallery menu.

For more chart style choices, check out all the other commands in the Gallery menu. They are only available when working with a chart.

Gallery⇨3-D Bar

This command changes the current chart into a 3-D bar chart.

Minimum mouse motion

Ample info

A 3-D bar chart is yet another way to help you display the comparison of two or more series of data at a specific moment in time. When using this command, the 3-D Bar dialog box displays several samples of 3-D charts for you to choose from. To choose a new style for your chart, just double-click the one you want from the samples in the dialog box.

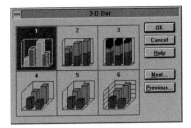

The following list describes each sample chart in the dialog box:

- Dialog box sample number one is a standard 3-D bar chart.

- Dialog box sample number two is a 3-D stacked bar chart.

- Dialog box sample number three is 3-D 100% stacked bar chart.

- Dialog box sample number four is a 3-D bar chart with side-by-side *series* and front-to-back *categories*.

- Dialog box sample number five is a 3-D bar chart with side-by-side *series* and front-to-back *categories* with vertical *gridlines*.

- Dialog box sample number six is a 3-D bar chart with side-by-side series and front-to-back categories with both vertical and horizontal gridlines.

Extra info

You can also change the chart's type by clicking a graph button in the toolbar.

For more chart style choices, check out all the other commands in the Gallery menu. They are only available when working with a chart.

Gallery ⇨ 3-D Line

This command changes the current chart into a 3-D line chart.

Minimum mouse motion

Ample info

Use a fancy 3-D line chart to show the difference between series of data over a long period of time. When using this command, the 3-D Line dialog box displays several samples of 3-D charts for you to choose from. To choose a new style for your chart, just double-click the one you want from the samples in the dialog box.

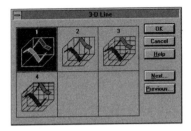

The following list describes each sample chart in the dialog box:

- Dialog box sample number one is a standard 3-D line chart.

- Dialog box sample number two is a 3-D line chart with vertical *gridlines*.

- Dialog box sample number three is a 3-D line chart with horizontal and vertical gridlines.

- Dialog box sample number four is a 3-D line chart with horizontal and vertical gridlines, but the scaling is *logarithmic*.

Extra info

 Clicking the Next or Previous button in the 3-D Line dialog box shows samples of the different chart styles. You can accomplish the same task by choosing a different chart style command from the Gallery menu, but using the dialog box buttons is faster.

 Highlight the cells in the spreadsheet first and then click the New Chart button in the toolbar.

Works uses the selected data from the spreadsheet's cells for its new chart.

 For more chart style choices, select another command from the Gallery menu. This menu is only available when you're working with a chart.

Gallery ⇨ 3-D Pie

This command changes the current chart into a 3-D pie chart.

Minimum mouse motion

Ample info

When using this command, the 3-D Pie dialog box displays several samples of 3-D charts for you to choose from. To choose a new style for your chart, just double-click the one you want from the samples in the dialog box.

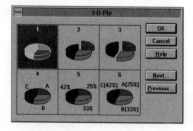

The following list describes each sample chart in the dialog box:

- Dialog box sample number one is a standard 3-D pie chart.

- Dialog box sample number two is a 3-D pie chart with one slice exploded.

- Dialog box sample number three is a 3-D pie chart with all the slices exploded.

- Dialog box sample number four is a standard 3-D pie chart with *category labels*.

- Dialog box sample number five is a 3-D pie chart with *data labels* as percentages only.

- Dialog box sample number six is a standard 3-D pie chart with category labels and data labels.

Extra info

You can also change the chart's type by clicking a graph button in the toolbar.

For more chart style choices, check out all the other commands in the Gallery menu. They are only available when working with a chart.

Gallery⇨Area

This command changes the current chart into an area chart.

Ample info

Area charts are similar to stacked line charts. They both show the changes and comparisons of several data series over a period of time, but the area chart emphasizes the amount of changes and similarities that occur in the data by displaying the cumulative totals in a color fill. When using this command, the Area dialog box displays several samples of charts for you to choose from. To choose a new style for your chart, just double-click the one you want from the samples in the dialog box.

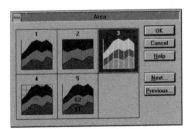

The following list describes each sample chart in the dialog box:

- Dialog box sample number one is a standard area chart.
- Dialog box sample number two is a 100% area chart.
- Dialog box sample number three is a standard area chart with *droplines*.
- Dialog box sample number four is a standard area chart with horizontal and vertical *gridlines*.
- Dialog box sample number five is a standard area chart with *data labels*.

Extra info

Clicking the Next or Previous button in the Area dialog box shows samples of the different chart styles. You can accomplish the same task by choosing a different chart style command from the Gallery menu, but using the dialog box buttons is faster.

You must create a chart by using the Tools⇨Create New Chart command in a spreadsheet before you can change a chart's style with a command from the Gallery menu.

For more chart style choices, check out all the other commands in the Gallery menu. They are only available when working with a chart.

Gallery⇨Bar

This command changes the current chart into a bar chart.

Minimum mouse motion

Ample info

A bar chart is a graphical display of a comparison of two or more series of data at a specific moment in time. Here's a delectable example — the number of times a vegetarian chews his or her food (savoring each bite, no doubt) at dinnertime compared to the number of times a steak-eater chews. When using this command, the Bar dialog box displays several samples of charts for you to choose from. To choose a new style for your chart, just double-click the one you want from the samples in the dialog box.

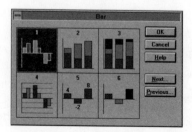

The following list describes each sample chart in the dialog box:

- Dialog box sample number one is a good, old-fashioned bar chart.

- Dialog box sample number two is a stacked bar chart.

- Dialog box sample number three is a 100% bar chart.

- Dialog box sample number four is a bar chart with horizontal *gridlines*.

- Dialog box sample number five is a bar chart with *data labels*.

- Dialog box sample number six is a bar chart with only one *series*.

Extra info

 Highlight the cells in the spreadsheet first and then click the New Chart button in the toolbar.

Works uses the selected data from the spreadsheet's cells for its new chart.

 For more chart style choices, check out all the other commands in the <u>G</u>allery menu. They are only available when working with a chart.

Gallery⇨Combination

This command changes the current chart into a combination (mixed) chart.

Minimum mouse motion

Ample info

A mixed or combination chart is a graphical display of two chart types together. A combination chart can emphasize the difference in a multiple data *series*. For example, you may use a bar chart to show this year's sales, with a line chart overlapping the bar chart showing next year's projected sales. When using this command, the Combination dialog box displays several samples of charts for you to choose from. To choose a new style for your chart, just double-click the one you want from the samples in the dialog box.

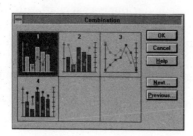

The following list describes each sample chart in the dialog box:

- Dialog box sample number one is a mixed bar and line chart in which the first series is the chart's bars and a second series is the chart's lines.

- Dialog box sample number two is a mixed bar and line chart (just like sample one) with a right vertical axis.

- Dialog box sample number three is a combination line chart only with a first and second series and a right vertical axis.

- Dialog box sample number four is a mixed Hi-Lo-Close chart (a special three series chart) with a right vertical axis.

Extra info

Clicking the Next or Previous button in the Combination dialog box shows samples of the different chart styles. You can accomplish the same task by choosing a different chart style command from the Gallery menu, but using the dialog box buttons is faster.

You must create a chart first by using the Tools⇨Create New Chart command in a spreadsheet before you can change a chart's style with a command from the Gallery menu.

For more chart style choices, check out all the other commands in the Gallery menu. They are only available when working with a chart.

This command changes the current chart into a line chart.

Minimum mouse motion

Ample info

A line chart is a good chart to use if you are trying to show the difference among several data series over a long period of time. These charts show patterns and can predict trends. When using this command, the Line dialog box displays several samples of charts to choose from. To choose a new style for your chart, just double-click the one you want from the samples in the dialog box.

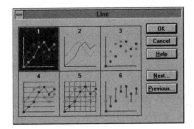

The following list describes each sample chart in the dialog box:

- Dialog box sample number one is a standard line chart.

- Dialog box sample number two is a line chart without any markers.

- Dialog box sample number three is a line chart with markers but no lines.

- Dialog box sample number four is a line chart with horizontal *gridlines*.

- Dialog box sample number five is a line chart with horizontal and vertical gridlines.

- Dialog box sample number six is a Hi-Lo chart.

Extra info

You can also change the chart's type by clicking a graph button in the toolbar.

For more chart style choices, check out all the other commands in the Gallery menu.

Gallery ⇨ Pie

This command changes the current chart into a pie chart.

Minimum mouse motion

Ample info

Pie charts show the proportional relationships (slices) of the data in one (whole pie) series. For instance, you can use a pie chart to show the proportions of each type of chemical (the size of each slice) used in the fertilizer spray (whole pie) for your lawn. When using this command, the Pie dialog box displays several samples of charts for you to choose from. To choose a new style for your chart, just double-click the one you want from the samples in the dialog box.

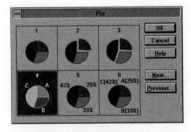

The following list describes each sample chart in the dialog box:

- Dialog box sample number one is a standard pie chart.

- Dialog box sample number two is a standard pie chart with the first slice exploded. The first slice is the first one located after 12 o'clock, if you vision the pie as a clock.

- Dialog box sample number three is a pie chart with all slices exploded.

- Dialog box sample number four is a pie chart with *category labels*

- Dialog box sample number five is a pie chart with percentage *data labels*.

- Dialog box sample number six is a pie chart with category and data labels.

Extra info

 Clicking the <u>N</u>ext or <u>P</u>revious button in the Pie dialog box shows samples of the different chart styles. You can accomplish the same task by choosing a different chart style command from the <u>G</u>allery menu, but using the dialog box buttons is faster.

 Highlight the cells in the spreadsheet first and then click the New Chart button in the toolbar.

Works uses the selected data from the spreadsheet's cells for its new chart.

 For more chart styles, check out all the other commands in the <u>G</u>allery menu. They are only available when working with a chart.

Gallery⇨Radar

This command changes the current chart into a radar chart.

Ample info

Radar charts are similar to line charts, but the data from several series is plotted on several category axes (spokes) around a common center point. This chart shows graphically the differences between the total values of data in several series. When using this command, the Radar dialog box displays several samples of charts for you to choose from. To choose a new style for your chart, just double-click the one you want from the samples in the dialog box.

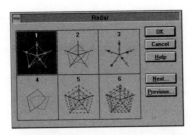

The following list describes each sample chart in the dialog box:

- Dialog box sample number one is a standard radar chart.

- Dialog box sample number two is a radar chart with the lines only.

- Dialog box sample number three is a radar chart with the markers only.

- Dialog box sample number four is a radar chart with lines but no axes.

- Dialog box sample number five is a radar chart with lines, *gridlines*, and axes.

- Dialog box sample number six is a radar chart with lines, axes, and *logarithmic* gridlines.

Extra info

You can also change the chart's type by clicking a graph button in the toolbar.

For more chart style choices, choose another command from the Gallery menu. This menu is available when working with a chart.

Gallery⇨Set Preferred Chart

Choose this command to make all new charts match the chart type of the current one.

Ample info

Suppose you have to make 25 bar charts for a slide presentation. To make a bar chart your *default* chart, create a bar chart from the Gallery menu and then choose the Set Preferred Chart command from the Gallery menu.

Gallery⇨Stacked Line

This command changes the current chart into a stacked line chart.

Ample info

You can use a stacked line chart to compare the sums of data from different categories — each data sum creates a different series for the chart. Call your friendly actuary to find out when to use this chart. When using this command, the Stacked Line (what a great name for a dance club) dialog box displays several samples of charts to choose from. To choose a new style for your chart, just double-click the one you want from the samples in the dialog box.

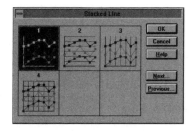

Look at the following list to see what the sample charts in the dialog box mean:

- Dialog box sample number one is a standard stacked line chart.

- Dialog box sample number two is a stacked line chart with horizontal *gridlines*.

- Dialog box sample number three is a stacked line chart with vertical gridlines.

- Dialog box sample number four is a stacked line chart with vertical and horizontal gridlines.

Extra info

You must create a chart first by using the Tools⇨Create New Chart command in a spreadsheet before you can change a chart's style with a command from the Gallery menu.

For more chart types, check out all the other commands in the Gallery menu. This menu is only available when working with a chart.

Gallery⇨X-Y (Scatter)

This command changes the current chart into an X-Y, or scatter chart.

Minimum mouse motion

Ample info

You can use scatter charts to show the difference between data in two sets of values. For example, the number of tires you puncture compared to the number of nails found in your driveway. When using this command, the X-Y (Scatter) dialog box displays several samples of charts for you to choose from. To choose a new style for your chart, just double-click the one you want from the samples in the dialog box.

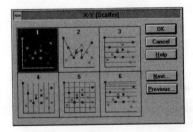

The following list describes each sample chart in the dialog box:

- Dialog box sample number one is a standard X-Y chart.

- Dialog box sample number two is an X-Y chart with the markers connected.

- Dialog box sample number three is an X-Y chart with horizontal *gridlines*.

- Dialog box sample number four is an X-Y chart with vertical gridlines.

- Dialog box sample number five is an X-Y chart with horizontal and vertical gridlines.

- Dialog box sample number six is an X-Y chart with horizontal *logarithmic* gridlines.

Extra info

 Clicking the <u>N</u>ext or <u>P</u>revious button in the X-Y (Scatter) dialog box shows samples of the different chart styles. You can accomplish the same task by choosing a different chart style command from the <u>G</u>allery menu, but using the dialog box buttons is faster.

 Highlight the cells in the spreadsheet first and then click the New Chart button in the toolbar.

Works uses the selected data from the spreadsheet's cells for its new chart.

 For more chart style choices, check out all the other commands in the <u>G</u>allery menu. They are only available when working with a chart.

Help⇨About Microsoft Works

This command displays all of the software's copyright information, its version number, and its serial number in a dialog box.

Extra info

 If you ever need to call Microsoft and you can't find the version or serial number of your Works program, choose <u>A</u>bout Microsoft Works from the <u>H</u>elp menu.

Help⇨Basic Skills

If you are a beginning Windows user, this command teaches you the basics of the Windows program. Click the search buttons or use the vertical scroll bar to find the topic you want to read about. Double-click the control box icon (the box at the upper-left corner of the help window) to close the overview.

Minimum mouse motion

Hot key hysteria

Opens a Help overview of the current document.

Help ⇨ Contents

You can search through all aspects of the Works program with
this command. Click the search buttons or use the vertical scroll
bar to find the topic you want to read about. Double-click the
control box icon (the box at the upper-left corner of the Help
window) to close the overview.

Minimum mouse motion

Help ⇨ Cue Cards

The Cue Cards are Microsoft's answer to a Help window that can
always be kept in view (on top) when working on a document.
The other Help menu commands use windows that can get
hidden when you click on the document to active it again.
Another important feature of the Cue Cards is that the card's Help
content changes automatically when switching between the
different types of Works documents. To use the cards, read the
prompts in the window. It's foolproof.

Minimum mouse motion

Help⇨How to Use Help

Help yourself! Use the How to Use Help command from the Help menu to help you learn how the Works Help dialog box can help you do work in Works. Double-click the control box icon (the box at the upper-left corner of the Help window) to close the overview. (Fans of Joyce's *Finnegans Wake* should have no trouble with the two preceding sentences.)

Minimum mouse motion

Help⇨(module) Overview

This command gives an overview of the Works module that is currently open and active. For example, if the spreadsheet is active, then the command is Help⇨Spreadsheet overview. Click the search buttons or use the vertical scroll bar to find the topic you want to read about. Double-click the control box icon (the box at the upper-left corner of the Help window) to close the overview.

Minimum mouse motion

Hot key hysteria

Help⇨Search for Help on

This command allows you to click the search buttons or use the vertical scroll bar to find the topic you want to read about from an alphabetical index. Double-click the topic in the list to see more information about it. When you are finished, double-click the control box icon (the box at the upper-left corner of the Help window) to close the overview.

Minimum mouse motion

Help⇨Tutorial

You can view a complete tutorial about Microsoft Works with this command. It's like going to the movies — almost. When you finish with your popcorn, click the Exit sign — and don't forget to deposit your trash in the marked receptacles when exiting.

Minimum mouse motion

Hot key hysteria

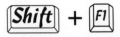

Insert⇨Bookmark Name

This command inserts a bookmark into a word processor document at the cursor location.

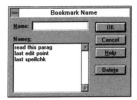

Ample info

Put the cursor in the location where you want to add a bookmark (in your word processor document). Choose the Bookmark Name command from the Insert menu. Type a Name for the bookmark in the dialog box and click OK. Each bookmark you insert into your document goes into the Names list of the dialog box. When you no longer need a bookmark, highlight it in the Names list and click the Delete button.

Extra info

 You can use a bookmark to mark the end of an edited or proofed section in a long document. The next time you open the document, use the Edit⇨Go To command to go to that bookmark to start editing where you left off.

 After bookmarks are named and inserted with the Insert⇨Bookmark Name command, use the Edit⇨Go To command (or just press F5) to find them later.

 You can only insert bookmarks into word processor documents. To mark different areas in a spreadsheet, use the Insert⇨Range Name command.

Insert⇨Chart

You can use this command to insert a chart into a Works word processor document or database form.

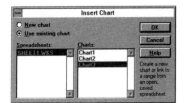

Ample info

From the Insert Chart dialog box, first decide whether to insert a New Chart or Use an existing chart.

If you select the New chart radio button and click OK, an information dialog box tells you what to do when the new chart's mini-spreadsheet is placed in your document. Click OK to finish inserting the mini-spreadsheet. Type in your cell values, highlight a cell range, and click the chart icon button in the lower-left corner of the mini-spreadsheet to complete your new chart.

To add an existing chart to your document, first click the Use existing chart radio button. Then select a spreadsheet name from the Spreadsheets list, followed by double-clicking a chart name in the Charts list.

Extra info

Use the Cut or Copy toolbar buttons to move or copy a selected chart to the Windows Clipboard. Then insert the chart into the document of any Windows application that allows you to use the Edit⟶Paste command — and most win-apps do.

The maximum number of charts that a spreadsheet can hold is eight, but you can open new spreadsheets to insert more charts.

Before you can insert an existing chart into your word processor document or database form, you must create one with the Tools⟶Create New Chart command in your spreadsheet.

Insert⟶ClipArt

This command opens the Works ClipArt Gallery application from a word processor document or database form.

Ample info

The ClipArt Gallery searches your computer's hard disk for images that can be inserted into your document and lets you choose them from a display of *thumbnail* pictures listed in the different categories that you create.

When you open the Microsoft ClipArt Gallery dialog box, just double-click a thumbnail picture to insert it into your document or form. To change a thumbnail or add new ones to the list box, click the Options button.

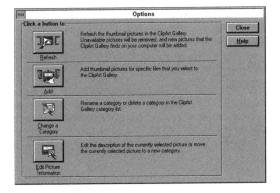

In the Options dialog box, you can Refresh the thumbnail pictures that are already in the ClipArt Gallery (refreshing makes the Clipart Gallery read the files again to create new thumbnails when you have changed or deleted them); Add more thumbnail pictures to the Gallery; Change a Category of thumbnails; or Edit Picture Information for a picture selected from the thumbnail list. Click Close to return to the Microsoft ClipArt Gallery dialog box.

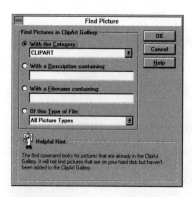

Clicking the Find button opens the Find Picture dialog box where you can search for pictures to add to the ClipArt Gallery. Click one of the radio buttons in the dialog box and type its search criteria, or choose a search option from its drop-down list. Click OK or press Enter to begin your search. The search results are displayed in the ClipArt Gallery's list box as thumbnails, so just double-click one to insert it into a document or form.

Extra info

When searching for the ClipArt files that are packaged with the Works program, look for files with a WMF extension in the C:\MSWORKS\CLIPART directory. This is probably the directory that Works used to install them.

Don't forget that the Paste command from the Edit menu can insert a picture that is located in the Windows Clipboard.

You can use the Insert⇨Object command to place *linked* pictures in your document.

See more about the WordArt Gallery in Chapter 25 in *Microsoft Works 3 For Windows For Dummies*.

Insert⇨Database Field

This command inserts field placeholders into your document. The placeholders reference the fields in a database so that you can print form-type documents. (Old-timers call this "mail merging.")

Ample info

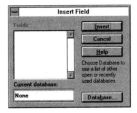

When the Insert Field dialog box first appears, the Fields list is always empty. Click the Data*b*ase button to open the Choose Database dialog box.

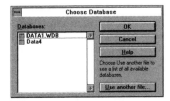

You can double-click a database that uses the fields you need for your document from the *D*atabases list, or you can click *U*se another file to use other database documents created by other database programs.

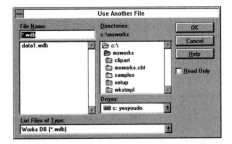

You've probably seen the Use Another File dialog box before. It's the same as the Save dialog box or Open Existing File dialog box found in the *F*ile menu. Locate another database file (*.wdb) to use and double-click it.

When you return to the Insert Field dialog box, the Fields box lists the fields of the chosen database. Double-click a field to insert it as a placeholder next to the cursor position in your document.

Extra info

Use the Insert⇨Database Field command to create form letters. These types of letters are individually addressed to match the addresses that you've listed in a database.

Don't change the text in a field placeholder or mess with the funny looking tent shaped characters that surround it. Doing so may prevent the placeholder from looking back to its database for the right data to insert in your form.

Once a document contains field placeholders, it can be printed normally, but first use the Print Preview command in the File menu to catch any mistakes in your form letter.

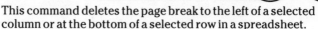

Insert⇨Delete Page Break

This command deletes the page break to the left of a selected column or at the bottom of a selected row in a spreadsheet.

Extra info

To create a page break, use the Insert⇨Page Break command.

Insert⇨Delete Record

This command deletes the current record in a database form.

Extra info

Press Ctrl+Z to bring back a deleted record.

To add a record to a database form, use the Insert⇨Record command.

Insert⇨Delete Record/Field

This command deletes a selected Record (row) or the Field (column) in a database list.

Extra info

When you delete a field in a database, you lose all the data for that field in every record.

Press Ctrl+Z to bring back a deleted record or field.

To add a record or a field to a database list, use the Insert⇨Record/Field command.

Insert⇨Delete Row/Column

This command deletes a selected Row or Column in a database report.

Extra info

You can press Ctrl+Z to restore any rows or columns that you accidentally delete.

To insert a row or column into a database report, select the Insert⇨Row/Column command.

Insert⇨Delete Selection

This command deletes the selected field name in a database form.

Extra info

You can press Ctrl+Z to restore a field that you accidentally delete.

To add a field to a database form, use the Insert⇨Field command.

This command opens Microsoft Draw. Use this application to create or open a drawing for insertion into your word processor or database form's page.

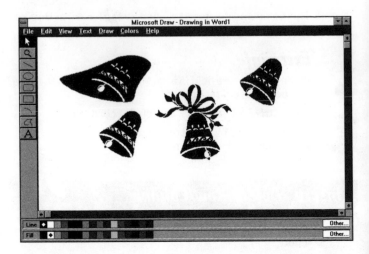

Ample info

When the Microsoft Draw program opens, click a drawing tool in the left side of the drawing area to start drawing, or choose the Import Picture command from the File menu to edit a drawing on a disk. The tools on the left side of the drawing window are described in order as follows:

- The Arrow tool is used to choose objects and move them.

- The Zoom tool magnifies the drawing for greater detail.

- The Ellipse tool draws an ellipse (or a circle if you press Shift while dragging).

- The Rounded Corner Rectangle tool draws a rounded rectangle (or rounded square if you press Shift while dragging).

- The Rectangle tool draws a rectangle (or square if you press Shift while dragging).

- The Arc tool draws an arc.

- The Freeform Draw tool draws a shape that matches your mouse movement.
- The Text tool places a line of text on your drawing.

Extra info

To edit an object's shape in a ClipArt picture, find another drawing program because the nodes that control the shape cannot be manipulated with the tools in Microsoft Draw.

You can insert drawings created from other Windows applications with the Insert⇨Object command.

Use the Format⇨Border command or the Insert⇨Rectangle command to add simple borders to your document.

Insert ⇨ Field

This command inserts a field name and data-entry box into a database form.

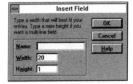

The Insert Field dialog box gives you an area to type in a Name and two areas to type the Width in characters and the Height in text lines for the data-entry boxes.

Minimum mouse motion

Click the Insert Field toolbar button. It's much faster than the Insert⇨Field command.

Insert⇨Field Entry

This command inserts a *field entry* into a database report.

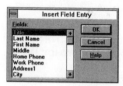

To add a new field entry, use the Insert Field Entry dialog box and double-click the database's field name from the Fields list.

Extra info

You can use the Field Name and Field Summary commands from the Insert menu to complete a database report.

See how database reports are made in Chapter 18 of *Microsoft Works 3 For Windows For Dummies*.

Insert⇨Field Name

This command inserts a *field name* into a database report.

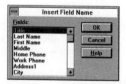

To add a field name to your form, double-click an item from the Fields list in the Insert Field Name dialog box.

Extra info

You can use the Field Entry and Field Summary commands from the Insert menu to complete a database report.

See how database reports are made in Chapter 18 of *Microsoft Works 3 For Windows For Dummies*.

Insert⇨Field Summary

This command inserts a *field summary row* into a database report.

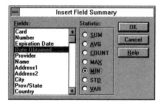

To insert a field summary into a report, click a Statistic radio button to choose a function task for the summary row, and then double-click a field name from the Fields list in the Insert Field Summary dialog box. When a summary is inserted, special statistics about the data in the spreadsheet can be printed with your report.

Ample info

The following describes each function from the Statistic list in the Insert Field Summary dialog box:

- SUM adds all the numbers in a field summary.

- AVG averages all the numbers in a field summary.

- COUNT counts the number of data entries in a field summary.

- MAX finds the largest number in a field summary.

- MIN finds the smallest number in a field summary.

- STD calculates the *standard deviation* for a field summary.

- VAR calculates the *variance* for a field summary.

Extra info

You can use the Field Entry and Field Name commands from the Insert menu to complete a database report.

See how you can make database reports in Chapter 18 of *Microsoft Works 3 For Windows For Dummies*.

You can add *Footnotes* to a word processor document using this command.

Ample info

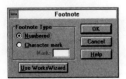

First place the cursor in your word processor document in the spot where you want the footnote. Choose a Numbered or Character mark footnote from the Footnote dialog box. If you choose to add a character to the footnote, type the character in the Mark box. Click OK to add the footnote to your document.

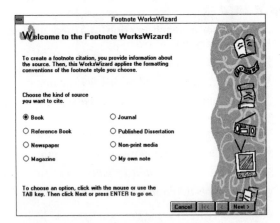

If you want to use the Microsoft Works footnote design, click the Use WorksWizard button and follow the Footnote WorksWizard's instructions in the dialog box.

Extra info

To use a crazy footnote character like the ones that avant garde
magazines use, open the Windows Character Map application by
selecting the File⇨Run command from the Windows program
manager, type **CHARMAP**, click OK, and then pick a weird
character to copy to the Clipboard. (See *Windows For Dummies*
for more information about character mapping.) Return to your
Works word processor document and choose the Footnote
command from the Insert menu. Select Character mark and then
click the Mark box in the Footnote dialog box. Use the Edit⇨Paste
command to paste the Clipboard character in the Mark box. Click
OK to see your cool footnote inserted into your document.

Insert⇨Function

This command lets you choose from a list of all the Functions
available in a Works spreadsheet.

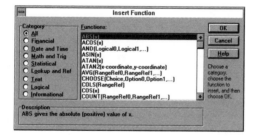

Ample info

Double-click a Function to insert it into your spreadsheet. If you
want to select a function from a single category, click a different
radio button from the Category list and then double-click the
Function you want to insert. A description of the function appears
in the lower part of the Insert Function dialog box.

Extra info

Most beginners don't use these spreadsheet functions, so don't
feel compelled to learn them right away. Simple math functions
are the ones used the most — like * (multiply), / (divide), + (add),
- (subtract), and the Autosum button in the toolbar.

Don't forget that a different Description appears at the bottom of the dialog box for each function highlighted in the Functions list box. To receive more information about a function, click to highlight it and then click the Help button in the Insert Function dialog box.

 For ultra-ultimate function descriptions, refer to Chapter 13 of *Microsoft Works 3 For Windows For Dummies.*

Insert⇨Label

This command inserts a new label into a database form at the position of the cursor.

Ample info

Type a Label Name in the Label Entry dialog box and click OK to add the new label to a form. After insertion, you can reposition a form's label by clicking it and then dragging it with your mouse.

Labels are used to describe the data entries in a database form more completely. This makes the data that you enter more consistent, which in turn makes the database more useable for detailed queries.

Extra info

 The only way to resize a label is by increasing or decreasing its text size with the Font Size drop-down menu in the toolbar. To make a border around the label, use the Format⇨Border command.

 If you want to create a movable, resizable, and customizable border around a label, you can create one with the Insert⇨Rectangle command. Reposition and size the rectangle by dragging one of its handles with the mouse, and then use the Format⇨Border command to customize its thickness and fill color.

Insert⇨Note-It

This command opens the Works Note-It accessory, which allows you to place a stick-it note in a word processor document or database form.

Ample info

This kind of note never falls off or gets lost. You can move it around by dragging it, or you can delete it using the Delete key at any time. The contents of the note stay hidden until you double-click it. Don't look for the contents to appear on the note because they don't; they show up as a separate small text box toward the top of the form or document.

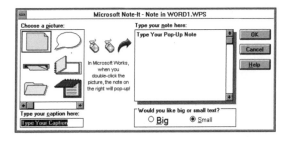

You can Choose a picture for the Note-It by clicking the one you want. Use the horizontal scroll bar to scan a wide variety of other Note-It styles. Type your caption that appears under the Note-It, and then Type your note that pops up when you double-click the Note-It. Click OK to insert the Note-It into your form or document.

Extra info

You can cut or copy a Note-It from one database form or word processor document using the Edit⇨Cut or Edit⇨Copy command and then paste it into another database or word processor document with the Edit⇨Paste command.

When a Note-It is created, you can edit it by clicking it and then choosing the Edit⇨Microsoft Note-It Object⇨Edit command.

Insert⇨Object

You can use this command to either choose or create an object to insert into your word processor document or database form. After you insert the object, double-click it to open the original Windows application that the object was created in. Edit the object and then close its application. The changed object appears in your form or document.

Ample info

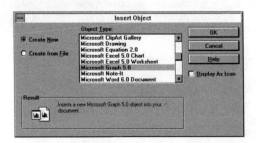

In the Insert Object dialog box, select the Create New radio button and choose an Object Type. Then click OK to open a Windows application to create the object. When you are finished, close the application and the new object is inserted into your document or form.

If you click the Create from File radio button, the dialog box changes so that you can find an object file on your disk and then insert it into your document or form with a click of the OK button. If the Link box is clicked, the object file that's inserted becomes *linked*. This means that if you ever change the object file, the object in your document or form is updated automatically to reflect the file's changes.

Extra info

Double-clicking an inserted object opens the application that it was created in.

Your applications may slow to a crawl if two or more Windows applications are opened together while editing inserted objects in Works.

You can use the Edit⇨Paste Special command to insert linked objects in Works.

Insert⇨Page Break

This command inserts a page break, which starts a new page in any Works document.

Hot key hysteria

Ctrl + **Enter**   (only available in a word processor document)

Extra info

You can use page breaks to control the page flow of your documents. To put a chart on its own separate page in your word processor document, use the Insert⇨Page Break command, insert a chart with the Insert⇨Chart command, and then use the Insert⇨Page Break command again.

Use the Format⇨Paragraph command to control the flow of paragraph text between pages in a word processor document rather than the Insert⇨Page Break command. This keeps the chances of creating extra blank pages to a minimum, and it makes your document style more consistent.

Insert⇨Range Name

You can use this command for naming ranges (selected cell areas) in a spreadsheet.

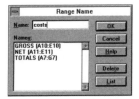

Ample info

Highlight the cells that compose the range in your spreadsheet. Choose the Range Name command from the Insert menu. Type a Name for the range in the dialog box and click OK. Each range you put in a document is added to the Names list of the Range Name dialog box. When you no longer need a range, highlight it in the Names list and then click the Delete button.

The List button inserts the list of the range Names and cell references from the dialog box and places them next to the active cell in a spreadsheet.

Extra info

Use the Edit⇨Go To command to find a range in a spreadsheet.

The Insert⇨Spreadsheet/Table command shows the list of range names in a spreadsheet. Double-click a name to insert it as a spreadsheet or table into your word processor document.

Insert⇨Record

This command adds a new record in a database form.

Minimum mouse motion

Click the Insert Record toolbar button to quickly add a new record to your form.

Extra info

To delete a record in a database form, use the Insert⇨Delete Record command.

Insert⇨Record/Field

This command adds a new Record (row) or a Field (column) in a database list.

Extra info

To delete a *record* or *field* in a database list, use the Insert⇨Delete Record/Field command.

The Insert⇨Record/Field command inserts a new record above a selected record (row) and a new field to the left of a selected field (column).

Insert⇨Rectangle

This command adds a rectangle around groups of elements in your database form.

Extra info

After you insert a rectangle into a form, you can drag from the middle of the rectangle to move it, drag from any corner to size it, and then use the Format⇨Border command to change the line and fill properties.

The Format⇨Border command adds a border around one selected element, while the Insert⇨Rectangle command adds a border around groups of elements.

Insert⇨Row/Column

This command adds a Row or Column to a database report.

Minimum mouse motion

Click the Insert Record toolbar button to add a new row (record) to your report.

Extra info

The Insert⇨Row/Column command inserts a new row above a selected row or a new column to the left of a selected column.

To delete a row or column in a database report, select the Insert⇨Delete Row/Column command.

Insert⇨Special Character

This command inserts special characters into your document that can automatically control hyphenation, printing, and time functions in word processor or database form documents.

Ample info

Click the radio button of a function that you want, and then click OK to insert it into your document or form.

Extra info

The special characters do not print on paper.

Don't accidentally change an inserted special character in your document because the special code that it carries will prevent the character from doing its job.

Insert⇨Spreadsheet/Table

You can insert a spreadsheet or table into your word processor document or database form with this command.

Minimum mouse motion

Ample info

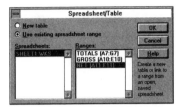

In the Spreadsheet/Table dialog box, you can choose to insert a New table or Use an existing spreadsheet range.

Select the New table radio button and then click OK to insert a mini-spreadsheet into the document. Type in your cell values, highlight a cell range, and click the chart button in the lower-left corner of the mini-spreadsheet to complete your new table.

To use an existing spreadsheet range, first click the Use existing spreadsheet range radio button. Then select a spreadsheet name from the Spreadsheets list and double-click a range name in the Ranges list to add the existing spreadsheet range to your document.

Extra info

Arrange your current display windows in Works with the Window⇨Tile command and then *drag and drop* objects between your database, word processor, and spreadsheet.

Drag an inserted spreadsheet or table to move it, or double-click it to edit it.

To insert a spreadsheet or table, you must first select the cells for your range in a spreadsheet and then name them with the Insert⇨Range Name command.

Insert⇨WordArt

This command opens another Microsoft accessory called WordArt, a graphical text editor. With this accessory, you can stretch, bend, color, and change text throughout a word processor document or database form.

Ample info

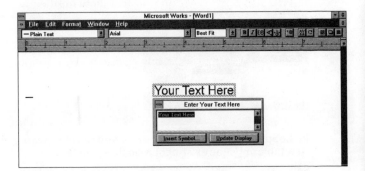

When you choose the Insert⇨WordArt command, the Enter Your Text Here dialog box appears. Type the text to edit in the text area of the dialog box. Click the Update Display button to apply the text characters in the dialog box to your document or form.

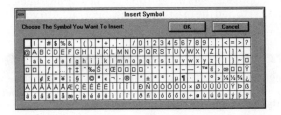

Click the Insert Symbol button in the Enter Your Text Here dialog box to open the Insert Symbol dialog box. Click the symbol that you want, and then click OK or press Enter to insert the symbol into the Enter Your Text Here dialog box. Click OK again to return to your document or form.

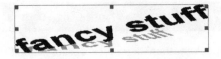

Click WordArt text to select it, which makes eight sizing handles appear around the WordArt object. Size the WordArt by dragging a handle, or use a toolbar button in the program to modify the text.

Extra info

Instead of boring you with lots of facts about the tools in WordArt, I recommend that you play around and experiment with them instead.

Double-click the WordArt text in your document or choose WordArt <u>O</u>bject from the <u>E</u>dit menu to edit a WordArt object.

Phone⇨Break

This communications command sends a special *break signal* to the computer that you're having a communications session with (called the remote computer). This signal stops the remote computer's current activity so that it can respond to other commands.

Extra info

The Phone <u>B</u>reak command can be especially handy when you've stopped the *download* process (receiving a file), but the remote computer is still *uploading* (sending you file data).

Phone⇨Dial

This command dials the current number of the Works communications file that is open.

Minimum mouse motion

Click the Easy Connect button if no number exists or if you want to change the current number in the Works Communications file.

Click the Dial/Hang-up button to either dial the current number of your communications file or to hang up (disconnect) when a communications session is finished.

Extra info

Don't use the Dial/Hang-up button in the communications toolbar when you're in the process of communicating with another computer — doing so may crash or stop the remote computer system.

Each time you use the Works communications program, Works prompts you to save the file. If you have saved the current communications file, you can open and reuse all of its settings (including the name and phone number) later.

Read about using the Phone⇨Easy Connect command to establish a current phone number in order to dial with the Phone⇨Dial command.

Phone⇨Dial Again

This command reestablishes a previous communications connection or it redials the current number.

Minimum mouse motion

Extra info

Read about the Phone⇨Easy Connect command to create or change a current phone number of a Works communications file.

Phone⇨Easy Connect

Choose from a list of previously called services (computers), or tell Works which new number to call with this command.

Minimum mouse motion

Ample info

The Easy Connect dialog box lists the last Services called — just double-click one to call it again. To call a new service (computer), enter its Phone number and Name of service in the text boxes.

Extra info

Previously-dialed numbers become listed at the bottom of the Phone menu. Instead of using the Phone⇨Easy Connect command and dialog box, just press Alt+P and then press the underlined number from the bottom of the Phone menu.

If you enter a new service Name and Phone number in the Easy Connect dialog box, you must save the current communications file before the new number appears in the Services list.

Read all about beginning a communications session in Part VII of *Microsoft Works 3 For Windows For Dummies*.

Phone⇨Pause

This command pauses the transfer of text from another computer so that it can be searched and read from the communications program's window.

Minimum mouse motion

Extra info

You can capture the text you're receiving *(on-line)* in a communications session with the Tools⇨Capture Text command and read it later *(off-line)* with the Works word processor. This prevents your eyes from crossing and cuts down the cost of your phone bills.

When you highlight text during a text file transfer, the communications session pauses. Click the Pause button in the toolbar to start receiving more text.

To capture the text coming from a service, use the Tools⇨Capture Text command.

Read more about transferring text files over a phone line in Part VII of *Microsoft Works 3 For Windows For Dummies*.

Settings⇨Communication

This command changes the settings of how data is sent from one computer to another using a modem.

Minimum mouse motion

Clicking the Communications Settings button is a little faster than choosing Communications from the Settings menu.

Clicking the 8-n-1 settings button from the communications toolbar is much faster than choosing the settings with the Settings⇨Communications command. This setting is the most common among computer bulletin board services.

Clicking the 7-e-1 settings button from the communications toolbar is also faster than choosing the settings with the Settings⇨Communications command. This setting is used often for communicating with large mainframes that supply data searching services.

Ample info

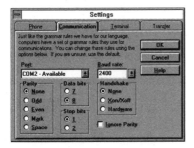

You should rarely need to change the Communication tab of the Settings dialog box. Sometimes, though not often, you may need to change Port selection when you add additional computer hardware, or you may need to raise the Baud rate if you purchase and install a higher speed modem.

Extra info

If you mess up the communication settings, just click the Cancel button in the Settings dialog box. If you click the OK button and save the wrong settings, just click the 8-n-1 Settings button or the 7-e-1 Settings button in the communications toolbar. (The 8-n-1 settings are the most widely used.)

Use the Settings⇨Modem command to automatically test your modem and set your modem's settings.

If you choose the wrong communication settings, a communications session won't work. If you're not sure about these settings, ask someone (but clicking the 8-n-1 Settings button or the 7-e-1 Settings button may solve the problem).

Settings⇨Modem

This setup command tells Works how to speak so that your modem can listen and understand.

Ample info

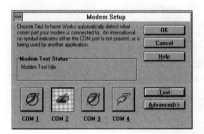

If you click the Test button in the Modem Setup dialog box, Works does all the setup work for you.

Click the Advanced button only if you have someone standing by your side who knows all about computer communications.

The command's dialog box even looks a little frightening.

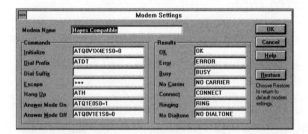

Extra info

Refer to the installation manual of your modem to find which modem settings you should enter in the Modem Settings dialog box's Commands section.

You can always click the Restore button in the Modem Settings dialog box to get your *default* settings back.

If you choose the wrong modem setting, your modem won't understand the commands that Works gives to it.

Settings⇨Phone

This settings command sets up how Works controls your
telephone.

Minimum mouse motion

Ample info

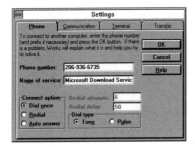

You can click a Connect option radio button to

- Dial once and then stop trying.

- Redial over and over until a connection is made.

- Auto answer your telephone when it rings.

Extra info

In the Dial type section of the Phone tab, choose Tone rather than
Pulse because most telephone hookups can now handle tone
dialing (not to mention the fact that it's much faster).

If the Phone number and the Name of service boxes are changed
in the Phone tab before you save the communications program
file, the new name and phone number is added to the Services list
in the Easy Connect dialog box.

Settings⇨Terminal

Choose settings for your terminal emulation with this command.

Minimum mouse motion

Ample info

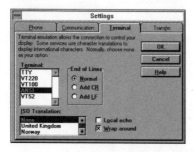

The most commonly-used Terminal setting in the Terminal tab of the Settings dialog box is ANSI. You may need the other settings if you're calling a mainframe. Check with your service before starting a communications session.

Extra info

If you choose the wrong terminal, a communications session will not work.

Settings⇨Transfer

This command gives you choices for the way (*transfer protocol*) computer files are sent (*uploaded* or *downloaded*) between two computers during a communications session.

Minimum mouse motion

Ample info

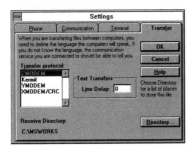

Works lists four types of Transfer protocols in the Transfer tab of the Settings dialog box. Click one to select it, but make sure the service you're calling has it, too. The most common is XModem/CRC. ZModem is also very popular because it is the fastest, you can transfer more than one file during a single transfer, and if you have problems with the phone line, you can call the service back and get the rest of the file without starting the whole transfer over again. YModem is okay, but use X or Z if you have the choice. Kermit is the transfer protocol you should use if you're having a communications session with a computer that is vastly different than yours — like a mainframe.

You can enter a larger Line Delay (tenths of a second) in the Text Transfers box if your computer is sending text faster than the receiving computer can read it.

Click the Directory button to choose which directory on a disk you want to store the files to be *downloaded* (received) from a computer service or bulletin board.

Extra info

Watch someone else call a computer service or bulletin board before you try it. You'll see that it's easier than it sounds, and you'll learn a lot by just watching.

Remember to click the <u>D</u>irectory button in the Trans<u>f</u>er tab of the Settings dialog box to set your receiving directory. If you forget to do this, it can be difficult to find the received file — with several thousand others on a large hard drive.

If you choose the wrong T<u>r</u>ansfer protocol, you won't be able to send or receive a file.

T<u>o</u>ols⇨*Calculate <u>N</u>ow*

Choose this command to recalculate your spreadsheet when it is in the manual calculation mode.

Hot key hysteria

Ample info

After you put your spreadsheet in manual calculation mode by choosing the <u>M</u>anual Calculation command from the T<u>o</u>ols menu, you must recalculate your spreadsheet manually by using the T<u>o</u>ols⇨Calculate <u>N</u>ow command or by pressing F9. If the T<u>o</u>ols⇨<u>M</u>anual Calculation command has a check mark next to it, the spreadsheet is in the manual calculation mode. Selecting the command again (removing the check mark) puts the spreadsheet in automatic calculation mode.

Extra info

 If a long spreadsheet is taking forever to recalculate automatically, you should put it in a manual calculation mode (T<u>o</u>ols⇨<u>M</u>anual Calculation) so that you can enter formulas and data in the spreadsheet without the recalculation wait after each entry.

T<u>o</u>ols⇨*C<u>a</u>ncel Recording*

This command cancels a script recording session in the Works communications program.

Extra info

To start a script recording session in the communications program, use the Tools⇨Record Script command.

Tools⇨Capture Text

You can save all the text coming from another computer during a communications session to a file by selecting this command.

Ample info

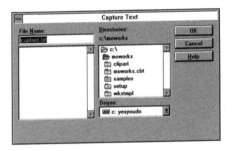

Use the Capture Text dialog box to choose a File Name, Drive, and Directory for your captured text file.

Extra info

Some text files that are captured during a communications session can become very large, so if you create one, don't forget to delete it from your disk later.

It's faster to open and view a communications text file later rather than reading it on-screen.

Choosing an existing text file from the File Name list in the Capture Text dialog box allows the newly captured text to erase the old text in the chosen file.

Tools⇨Create New Chart

This command creates a new chart from the selected cells in a spreadsheet.

Minimum mouse motion

Ample info

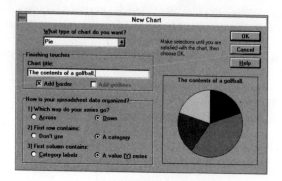

Answer the New Chart dialog box's three questions:

1. What type of chart do you want?

   Click the down arrow to choose a chart type.

2. What Finishing touches do you need to add?

   Choose some extra choices from this area of the dialog box.

3. How is your spreadsheet data organized?

   Click the appropriate radio buttons that tell your chart how the data is organized in the selected cells in the spreadsheet.

Extra info

To set the *default* chart type in the New Chart dialog box, use the Gallery⇨Set Preferred Chart command.

You can only have eight charts per spreadsheet in Works. If you already have eight charts that show the data in different ways from the same selected spreadsheet, you may want to select one of the eight with the View⇨Chart command and edit that one rather than create a new duplicate spreadsheet to add a ninth chart.

After you create a new chart, you can quickly change its style by choosing a command from the Gallery menu.

Creating charts is covered in Chapter 24 *of Microsoft Works 3 For Windows For Dummies.*

Tools⇨Create New Query

Use this command to select data criteria from a dialog box. The criteria is used to display only certain records in a database list or form view. The records that don't match the criteria are not deleted, just hidden.

Ample info

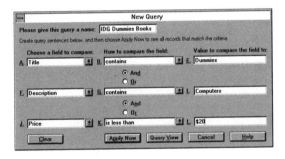

When the New Query dialog box opens, give the query a name by typing it in the appropriate text box. Choose the fields for the comparisons from the first column (A, F, and J) of drop-down boxes. The middle column (B, G, and K) of drop-down boxes is used for choosing how to compare the fields. Enter a value or text string criteria in the third column (E, I, and L) of text boxes. If you want a simple search, use only the text boxes in the first row. To see the records that match your criteria, click the Apply Now button, or click the Query View button to switch to the query view. To start all over, click the Clear button.

The example in the dialog box shows a query for a database of books. In plain English, this query reads as follows. "Show me all the books in my database whose title contains the word *Dummies,* and the description of the book contains the word *Computers,* and the price of the book is less than twenty dollars." Surprise! The result of this query shows every *Dummies* book that IDG Books publishes.

Extra info

Think of the rows of criteria in the New Query dialog box as parts of a long sentence — each part is connected with the conjunction *or* or *and*.

Choose only from the selections available in the drop-down boxes. Don't just type any ol' text in them or your query will not work.

To Name, Duplicate, or Delete a query, look at the corresponding commands in the Tools menu while working with a database form or list.

Read all about making queries for your database records in Chapter 17 of *Microsoft Works 3 For Windows For Dummies*.

Tools⇨ Create New Report

Choose this command to create a database *report*.

Ample info

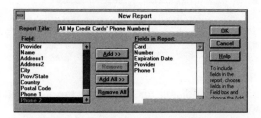

Type a Report Title in the New Report dialog box and then click a Field that you want added to the report, followed by a click on the Add button. All the fields you add become listed in the Fields in Report scroll box. After you choose all of the fields for your new report, click OK or press Enter.

Extra info

To Name, Duplicate, or Delete a report, look at the corresponding commands in the Tools menu when working with a database.

Read all about database reports in Chapter 18 of *Microsoft Works 3 For Windows For Dummies*.

Tools⇨Customize Toolbar

This command can add or delete toolbar buttons from any of the
Works toolbars — excluding the communications toolbar.

Ample info

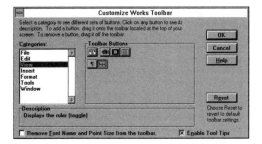

From the Customize Works Toolbar dialog box, click a category
from the Categories list to show a set of buttons that you can add
to your toolbar. Drag a button from the dialog box and drop it in
your toolbar to add it there. If you see a button in the toolbar that
you never use, just *drag and drop* it off the toolbar. Don't worry
about losing any toolbar buttons; just click the Reset button in
the dialog box to change the toolbar back to the *default*. If you're
not sure what a button does, just click it to reveal its Description
at the bottom of the dialog box. You can select or deselect the
button's Tool Tips, the Font drop-down list, and the Point Size
drop-down list by clicking the two check boxes at the bottom of
the dialog box.

Extra info

Take this command seriously; customizing the toolbars makes
using Works much faster.

You can also use the Tools⇨Options command to customize
Works.

Tools⇨Delete Chart

Delete a chart with this command.

Ample info

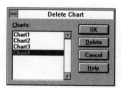

Click a chart that you want to delete in the Charts list, and then click the Delete button. Keep repeating the previous procedure to delete more charts. When you're finished with the Delete Chart dialog box, click OK.

Extra info

Only eight charts can be associated with one spreadsheet's data. To get more charts, either duplicate the spreadsheet or delete some charts from it.

The Edit⇨Undo command cannot bring back a deleted chart.

Tools⇨Delete Query

Delete a database query with this command.

Ample info

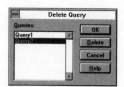

Click a query that you want to delete in the Queries list, and then click the Delete button. Repeat this procedure to delete more queries. When you're finished with the Delete Query dialog box, click OK.

Extra info

Don't delete a database query without checking its criteria first. You may be able to change it to a different query very easily. Changing a database query is faster than starting a new one from scratch.

The Edit⇨Undo command cannot bring back a deleted query.

Before you can delete a query, one must be created with the Tools⇨Create New Query command.

Chapter 17 of *Microsoft Works 3 For Windows For Dummies* tells you all about queries.

Tools⇨Delete Report

Delete a report from a database with this command.

Ample info

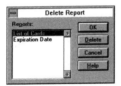

Click a report name from the Reports list that you want to delete and then click the Delete button. Repeat this procedure to delete more reports from a database. When you're finished with the Delete Report dialog box, click OK.

Extra info

The Edit⇨Undo command cannot bring back a deleted report.

Before you can delete a report, you must create one with the Tools⇨Create New Report command.

Chapter 18 of *Microsoft Works 3 For Windows For Dummies* is all about database reporting.

Tools⇨Dial This Number

Dial the highlighted telephone number in a Works document (for voice calls, not communication sessions) at any time by selecting this command from the Works menu bar.

Ample info

To dial a telephone number, highlight one from the document — or type a number to select — and then choose Dial This Number from the Tools menu.

Extra info

If you create a friends and family database, you can select a friend's number from the phone number field (column), and then use the Tools⇨Dial This Number command to dial it. (No more directory assistance charges!)

If you want to block out Call Waiting from a touch tone phone, enter ***70,** (star sign, seven, zero, comma) as a prefix to the number you are calling. Enter the prefix **1170,** if you are using a pulse dial phone.

This command is for voice calls only; use the communications program to make computer calls with your modem.

Tools⇨Duplicate Chart

Select a spreadsheet chart and duplicate it with this command.

Ample info

Click a chart in the Charts list that you want to duplicate, and then click the Duplicate button. Repeat this procedure to duplicate more charts. If you want a different name for the duplicate chart, type the new name in the Name text box. When you're finished with the Duplicate Chart dialog box, click OK.

Extra info

You can duplicate a chart and then change the duplicate to another type of chart using a command from the Gallery menu. This is a quick way to make two different styles of charts using identical spreadsheet data.

To create a chart, use the Tools⇨Create New Chart command from a spreadsheet's menu.

Tools⇨Duplicate Query

Select and duplicate a database query with this command.

Ample info

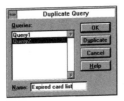

Click a query that you want to duplicate in the Queries list, and then click the Duplicate button. Repeat this procedure to duplicate more queries. If you want a different name for the duplicate, type the new name in the Name text box. When you're finished with the Duplicate Query dialog box, click OK.

Extra info

A quick way to make two queries with different criteria for use in a database is to duplicate a query and redefine the duplicate's search criteria.

To create a chart, use the Tools⇨Create New Query command from a database's menu.

Tools⇨Duplicate Report

You can select and duplicate a database report with this command.

Ample info

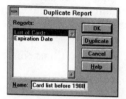

Click a report that you want to duplicate in the Reports list, and then click the Duplicate button. Repeat this procedure to duplicate more reports. If you want a different name for the duplicate, type the new name in the Name text box. When you're finished with the Duplicate Report dialog box, click OK.

Extra info

A quick way to make a second report to experiment with while still keeping the first one safe is to duplicate a report and then change the duplicate to try to make it better.

To create a chart, use the Tools⇨Create New Report command from a database's menu.

Tools⇨Edit Script

Choose a communication script to edit with this command.

Ample info

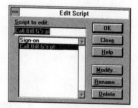

Select a script name from the Edit Script dialog box and click the Modify button.

In the Modify Script dialog box, you can Add, Replace, or Delete the Script Commands. Click Cancel to exit this dialog box, or click OK to save any changes you've added to your script. Once you are back in the Edit Script dialog box, you can click the Rename button.

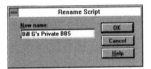

When the Rename Script dialog box opens, you can type a New name for the script. Click OK to save the new name.

Extra info

Using scripts can save you lots of time when keystroke actions are repetitive in a communications session.

Be careful when you modify a script because the wrong changes can make a connection to another computer halt or even crash.

You must first make a script with the Tools⇨Record Script command before you can find one to edit.

Use this command to set up text so that you can print on different
sizes of labels and envelopes. You can even use a database's
fields to automatically print envelope and address labels.

Ample info

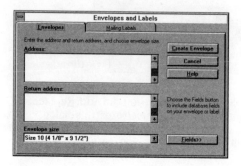

To create a custom-printed envelope, click the Envelopes tab in
the Envelopes and Labels dialog box. Type in the Address and the
Return Address. Choose the Envelope's size and click Create
Envelope to print the envelope.

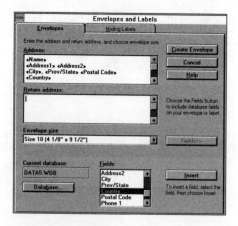

Click the Fields button in the Envelopes and Labels dialog box to
select fields from a chosen Database to Insert in the Address text
box. Click the Create Envelope button to print the data from the
address database fields on envelopes.

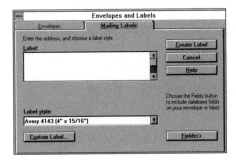

To create a custom-printed label, click the Mailing Labels tab in the Envelopes and Labels dialog box. Type the address in the Label text box and choose the correct Label style. Click the Create Label button to print the labels.

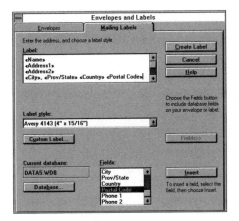

When you click the Fields button in the Mailing Labels tab, you can select Fields from a chosen Database to Insert into the Label text box. Clicking the Create Label button prints the address database field's data on labels. Click the Custom Label button if no Label style exists for the type of label you're using.

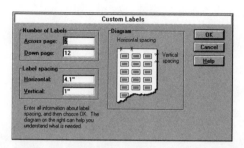

Use the Custom Labels dialog box to create a style that matches your odd-sized labels.

Extra info

To make the printing of labels easy, always buy a style of label that matches the list in the Label style drop-down list in the Mailing Labels tab of the Envelope and Labels dialog box.

Don't forget to turn on the printer and load it with the correct style of envelopes or labels.

You can waste lots of labels if the very first label is set up wrong in your printer. Check your printer's manual for tips.

Tools⇨Hyphenation

Use this command to hyphenate your paragraphs in a word processor document.

Ample info

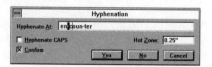

Insert the cursor at the spot where you want to begin hyphenating and choose the Tools⇨Hypenation command. When the Hyphenation dialog box opens, make sure the Confirm option is selected. Click the Yes button to confirm the hyphen's position or the No button to skip to the next hyphen's position in the word. Continue the confirmations for each hyphen of each word until the end of the documents or click Cancel to quit.

Extra info

Keep the Hot Zone in the Hyphenation dialog box at 0.25" or above. This keeps your text from getting too chopped up, but it makes the right margin a bit more uneven.

It's a good idea to keep the Confirm option selected (with an X in it). Your computer isn't always as smart as you may think.

Save your document (Ctrl+S) before applying hyphenation to it.

Tools⇨Manual Calculation

You can select this command to turn it on and then select it again to turn it off. When it's on, there is a check mark next to it in the Tools menu and you have to manually recalculate your spreadsheet if any formulas or values change. When turned off, Works recalculates a spreadsheet automatically.

Extra info

Press F9 to recalculate manually.

The Tools⇨Manual Calculation command works hand-in-hand with the Tools⇨Calculate Now command.

Tools⇨Name Chart

You can name a chart with this command when you're working with a spreadsheet or spreadsheet chart.

Ample info

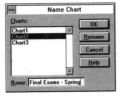

Click a chart from the <u>C</u>harts list, type a new <u>N</u>ame for it, and then click OK. To change the name of a chart, choose the chart from the <u>C</u>harts list, click the <u>R</u>ename button, type the new <u>N</u>ame, and click OK.

T<u>o</u>ols⇨Na<u>m</u>e <u>Q</u>uery

Use this command to name a query when working in a Works database.

Ample info

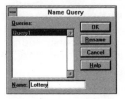

Click a query from the Queries list, type a new <u>N</u>ame for it, and then click OK. To change the name of a query, choose the query from the Queries list, click the <u>R</u>ename button, type the new <u>N</u>ame for it, and click OK.

T<u>o</u>ols⇨N<u>a</u>me Report

When working in a database, choose this command to name or rename a report.

Ample info

Click a report from the Reports list, type a new Name for it, and
then click OK. To change a name for a report, choose the report
from the Reports list, click the Rename button, type the new
Name for it, and click OK.

Tools⇨Options

Choose this command to control some important *default* options
in Works.

Ample info

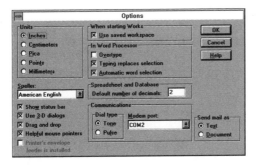

In the Options dialog box, select a measuring unit from the Units
section that Works can use for all of its measurements — such as
the rulers, page size, margin settings, column gutter widths,
borders, tabs, and so on.

The Speller drop-down menu shows other dictionaries that you
can select for your Spell Checker to use. The only other dictionary included with Works is British English.

It's best to leave the Show status bar, Use 3-D dialogs, Drag and
drop, and Helpful mouse pointers selected (marked with an X) if
you're a beginning Works user or are following this book closely.

If you use the File⇨Save Workspace command before closing the
Works program, the next time you start Works, its workspace will
reopen only if Use saved workspace is selected.

To customize how typing in the word processor is handled, select

- Overtype — If you want new text to replace the existing text
  instead of moving it over.

- Typing replaces selection — If you want the text that you type to replace any other text that's highlighted in your document.

- Automatic word selection — If you want Works to help you highlight text in whole-word increments when you highlight text from a sentence or paragraph.

Other options include a text box for entering the Default number of decimals shown in a spreadsheet or database, radio buttons to choose your phone's Dial type, a drop-down box to select your Modem port, and an option for sending modem mail as Text or a Works Document. Text is the best choice because bulletin board computer services use text files, not Works files.

Extra info

The Drag and drop option should be left on (marked with an X) in the Options dialog box because it is a key feature of the Works program.

The communications settings from the Settings⇨Modem command in a Works communications session are reflected in the Communications options in the Options dialog box.

Tools⇨Customize Toolbar is another command that can customize how Works works.

Tools⇨Paginate Now

This command tells the word processor to measure the length of a document and divide it into the proper number of pages.

Hot key hysteria

Ample info

Works repaginates (redetermines the place where the page breaks are) automatically when you type. You only have to use this command when you make drastic changes to page margins, line spacing, or other adjustments that affect the length of the total document.

Extra info

To adjust the amount of text in each document, set its margins with the File⇨Page Setup command and then use the Tools⇨Paginate Now command, or press F9.

You can tell Works where to end (break) a page by pressing Ctrl+Enter or the Insert⇨Page Break command.

Tools⇨Receive File

Use this command to tell Works to start receiving (downloading) a file when you are connected to another computer in a communications session.

Minimum mouse motion

Ample info

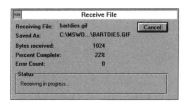

After you've called a computer service, follow the menus and commands to *download* a file. Then click the Receive File button on the toolbar. The Receive File dialog box shows you the status of the *downloading* process. The only other option in this dialog box is to click the Cancel button to stop the receiving process.

Extra info

If the Error Count in the Receive File dialog box is high (above 50 or 60), click Cancel and try again later. A high error count usually means that the phone connection is bad. Even though errors are caught with the X, Y, and Zmodem protocals, your downloading can take a long time.

You can use ***70,** (for a touch tone phone) or **1170,** (for a pulse phone) as your dialing prefix in the Works communication program settings (<u>S</u>ettings⇨<u>P</u>hone) before dialing another computer to disable the phone company's Call Waiting service. This prevents the phone from cutting off communications with another computer when somebody beeps in. Oh, by the way, the commas in the prefixes are used by Works as a pause before dialing the phone number.

 Never exit Works when you're in the middle of receiving a file; this can cause problems with the computer that you're connected to. Always use the Cancel button to stop receiving a file, log off the computer service, and then exit the Works program.

 To send (*upload*) a file over a phone line, see the T<u>o</u>ols⇨<u>S</u>end File command.

Tools⇨Record Script

This command allows you to start recording a script in a communications session.

Ample info

To start recording a script, choose which Type of script you want to record in the Record Script dialog box. Click the <u>S</u>ign-on radio button to record your actions when dialing and signing on to a computer service, or click <u>O</u>ther to record a repetitive task after you've signed on. Enter a Script <u>N</u>ame and then click OK to start recording.

Extra info

 Record a sign-on script if you call the same computer bulletin board service regularly. This script streamlines the repetitive *sign-on* process.

 If you're brave, you can edit a script with the T<u>o</u>ols⇨<u>E</u>dit Script command.

If you record a script while *on-line* with one computer service, it may not work when you're on-line with another service.

See the Tools⇨Cancel Recording and the Tools⇨Edit Script commands.

Tools⇨Send File

Use this command to tell Works to start sending *(uploading)* a file when you are connected to another computer in a communications session.

Minimum mouse motion

Ample info

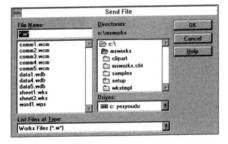

After you've called a computer service, follow the menus and commands to *upload* a file. Next, find the file you want to send using the Drives, Directories List, and File Type lists and click it in the File Name list to select it. Now click OK or press Enter to send the file to another computer.

Extra info

Keep all the files to be sent (uploaded) via modem in a place on your disk that you can find easily when faced with the Send File dialog box.

You can use ***70,** (for a touch tone phone) or **1170,** (for a pulse phone) as your dialing prefix in the Works communication program settings (Settings⇨Phone) before dialing another computer to disable the phone company's Call Waiting service. This prevents the phone from cutting off communications with another computer when somebody beeps in. Oh, by the way, the commas in the prefixes are used by Works for a pause before dialing the phone number.

Never exit Works when you're in the middle of receiving a file; this can cause problems with the computer that you're connected to. Always use the Cancel button to stop receiving a file, log off the computer service, and then exit the Works program.

To receive (download) a file over a phone line, see the Tools⇨Receive File command.

Tools⇨Send Text

While in a communications session with another computer, send your text files using this command.

Minimum mouse motion

Ample info

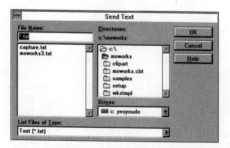

After you've called a computer service, follow the menus and commands to send (*upload*) a text file. Next, find the text file you want by using the Drives, Directories List, and File Type lists, and then click a file from the File Name list to select it. Click OK or press Enter to send the text to the service.

Extra info

Use the Tools⇨Send Text command when you send electronic mail or messages to a computer bulletin board service or to another computer.

You can use ***70,** (for a touch tone phone) or **1170,** (for a pulse phone) as your dialing prefix in the Works communication program settings (Settings⇨Phone) before dialing another computer to disable the phone company's Call Waiting service. This prevents the phone from cutting off communications with another computer when somebody beeps in. Oh, by the way, the commas in the prefixes are used by Works for a pause before dialing the phone number.

Never exit Works when you're in the middle of receiving a file; this can cause problems with the computer that you're connected to. Always use the Cancel button to stop receiving a file, log off the computer service, and then exit the Works program.

This command can usually be ignored. Refer to the Tools⇨Send File command and use it instead.

Tools⇨Sort Records

This command sorts the records (rows) in a database list or form.

Ample info

Choose the 1st Field to sort from the drop-down box in the Sort Records dialog box. Click a radio button to choose either an ascending (1,2,3; A,B,C) sort or a descending (5,4,3; Z,Y,X) sort. Click OK to sort your database records using the chosen field. For a more complete sort, you can use the 2nd Field and 3rd Field, too. The preceding figure shows what the dialog box looks like if you want your database records sorted by the State data first, the City data second, and the Last Name data third.

Extra info

Pressing Ctrl+Z undoes a sort.

See the Tools⇨Sort Rows command to sort the rows of a spreadsheet.

Tools⇨Sort Rows

This command sorts the rows in the active spreadsheet.

Ample info

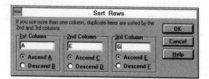

In the Sort Rows dialog box, choose the 1st Column you want to sort by typing its letter label in the text box. Click a radio button to choose either an ascending (1,2,3; A,B,C) sort or a descending (5,4,3; Z,Y,X) sort. Click OK to sort your rows using the chosen column. For a more complete sort, enter column labels in the 2nd Column and the 3rd Column text boxes. The preceding figure shows spreadsheet rows sorted by the values in column A first, column E second, and column G third.

Extra info

Pressing Ctrl+Z undoes a sort.

See the Tools⇨Sort Records command to sort the rows of a database form or list.

Tools⇨Spelling

Use this Works accessory to check the spelling of words in a Works word processor document, spreadsheet, or database.

Minimum mouse motion

Ample info

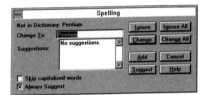

Press Ctrl+Home to move your cursor to the beginning of your document, and then click the Spelling button in the toolbar. The Spelling dialog box opens and the Spell Checker begins to scan your document for misspelled words. When it finds a misspelling, it highlights the word in your document, along with the Spell Checker's best guess for the correct word in the Change To text box. If this word is not correct, click the correct one from the Suggestions list. Words will only be listed in the Suggestions list if the Always Suggest option is checked in the lower-left corner of the dialog box. If no correct word is listed, type the correct word in the Change To box and then click the Change button. To correct all the other identical misspellings, click the Change All button.

If you know that the highlighted word is correct, click the Ignore button to move on, or click the Ignore All button to skip over every other identical word in the rest of the document. If you know a word is spelled correctly (like the word *Pentium* in the example), click the Add button to add it to the Spell Checker's dictionary so that the Spell Checker is taught its correct spelling. The Spell Checker continues looking through your document for more misspellings until it reaches the end. A dialog box appears to let you know that the Spell Checker is finished with its work.

Extra info

To ignore proper nouns like IDG, Beverly Ann, Fepseekoha, and IRS — click the Skip capitalized words box at the bottom of the Spelling dialog box.

If the Spell Checker finds a pair of identical words together, like *the the,* the Spelling dialog box gives you a <u>D</u>elete button to click to erase the highlighted extra one. The Checker also catches words that run together because a space is missing.

The Spell Checker will not catch the misspelling for *your* when you mean *you're* or *its* when you mean *it's.* Proofreading your document is the only way to catch these types of mistakes.

Tools⇨Thesaurus

You can use this Works accessory from the word processor to look up a synonym (a word with a similar meaning) for a selected word.

Ample info

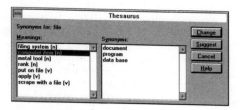

Highlight the word in the document that you want a synonym for. Choose the T<u>o</u>ols⇨<u>T</u>hesaurus command to open the Thesaurus dialog box. Choose the correct meaning of your word from the <u>M</u>eanings scroll box list and then double-click a synonym in the Synonyms list to replace your selected word in the document.

Extra info

In the Thesaurus dialog box, you can select different <u>M</u>eanings and then click the <u>S</u>uggest button to get more S<u>y</u>nonyms to choose from.

Excessively employing innumerable synonyms for words can make a document undecipherable.

Tools⇨Word Count

This command counts the number of words in a word processor document and gives you the results in a dialog box.

Extra info

If you select just a portion of a document, the Tools⇨Word Count command only counts the words in that selected portion.

View⇨All Characters

This command gives you a view of the nonprintable characters that Works uses to compose a word processor document.

Ample info

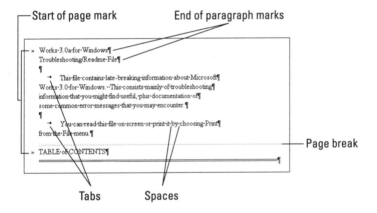

Start of page mark   End of paragraph marks

Page break

Tabs   Spaces

When you select View⇨All Characters, the document window shows the special characters that Works uses to show the end of paragraphs, blank spaces, tabs, the start of a page, and inserted breaks between pages.

Extra info

You should view the special characters when you're using a computer with a small screen because it's hard to tell if spacing is correct without them. The space marks (the dots in each space) help you see how many spaces are between each word.

If you want to see your document without all those special formatting characters and you have selected the <u>V</u>iew⇨<u>A</u>ll Characters command, you can use the <u>F</u>ile⇨Print Pre<u>v</u>iew command to preview a document, or select the <u>V</u>iew⇨<u>A</u>ll Characters command again to turn off the special character view.

<u>V</u>iew⇨Apply <u>Q</u>uery

This command applies your query to a database list or form.

Hot key hysteria

Ample info

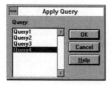

Double-click the query name to use from the Que<u>r</u>y list, and Works displays only the database records that match the query's criteria.

Extra info

You must first create a query before you can apply it to a database.

 See the T<u>o</u>ols⇨<u>C</u>reate New Query command to create a query for a database.

<u>V</u>iew⇨<u>C</u>hart

Choose a spreadsheet chart to view with this command.

Ample info

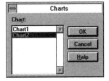

When the Charts dialog box appears, double-click a Chart name to view it.

Extra info

Only eight charts can be made for each spreadsheet in Works.

To make a chart in a spreadsheet, see the Tools➪Create New Chart command.

Using charts is explained in Chapter 23 of *Microsoft Works 3 For Windows For Dummies*.

View➪Display as Printed

When selected, this command shows your chart as if you're looking at the printed page. You can turn off this display feature by selecting View➪Display as Printed again.

Extra info

Because some colors look the same as others when printed in black and white, use the View➪Display as Printed option to check your color charts for the correct contrast before you print them on your black and white printer.

Using the File➪Print Preview command shows a color proof of your chart with no regard to the type of printer you have.

View➪Draft View

Switch to the draft view with this word processor command.

Ample info

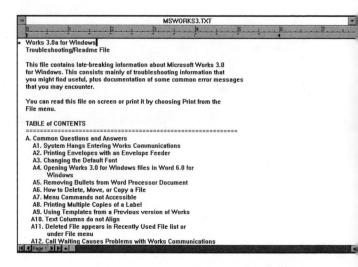

When you view a document in the draft view, the speed at which Works displays the document is increased dramatically because all the text is the same style and size; no headers, footers or columns are shown; no special paragraph or text formatting is displayed; and all objects in the document are displayed as rectangles.

Extra info

When working with long word processor documents, use the draft view to increase Works's display and processing speed.

Remember that the Alt+F+V keyboard stroke gives you a preview of your document.

The other two types of view commands in the word processor are View⇨Page Layout and View⇨Normal.

View⇨Field Lines

This command switches the *field lines* in a database form on and off.

Ample info

Date Entered:	(the date you entered data in this form)
Mr./Mrs./Ms.:	
First Name:	Last Name:
Company:	
Address Line 1:	
Address Line 2:	
City:	State:
Postal Code:	Country:
Phone:	Fax:
Credit Limit:	Account Rating:
# of Outlets:	

When the F<u>i</u>eld Lines command in the <u>V</u>iew menu is not selected, the field lines don't show.

Date Entered: _____	(the date you entered data in this form)
Mr./Mrs./Ms.: _____	
First Name: _____	Last Name: _____
Company: _____	
Address Line 1: _____	
Address Line 2: _____	
City: _____	State: _____
Postal Code: _____	Country: _____
Phone: _____	Fax: _____
Credit Limit: _____	Account Rating: _____
# of Outlets: _____	

When F<u>i</u>eld Lines in the <u>V</u>iew menu is selected (marked with a check mark), the field lines show.

Extra Info

Turn off the field lines in a form to display any lines or boxes that you made with Microsoft Draw.

Use the <u>I</u>nsert⇨Draw<u>i</u>ng command to use Microsoft Draw to draw custom field lines or boxes.

View⇨Footnotes

Select this command to show all the footnotes in a word processor document.

Ample info

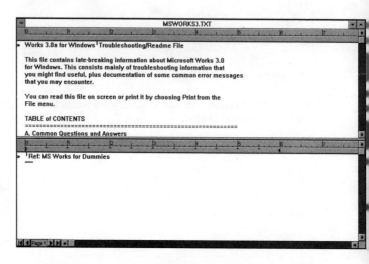

MSWORKS3.TXT

Works 3.0a for Windows Troubleshooting/Readme File

This file contains late-breaking information about Microsoft Works 3.0 for Windows. This consists mainly of troubleshooting information that you might find useful, plus documentation of some common error messages that you may encounter.

You can read this file on screen or print it by choosing Print from the File menu.

TABLE of CONTENTS
==
A. Common Questions and Answers

Ref: MS Works for Dummies

Page 1

The View⇨Footnotes command splits your document window into two window panes. The main text body of a document with the reference marks is in the top pane, and the footnoted text is in the bottom pane. You can click in either pane to edit, delete, copy, or move footnotes or reference marks.

Extra info

You can move the split bar between the two footnote panes in the document window by dragging it up and down with your mouse. When you finish working with footnotes, double-click the split bar to make the document into one window again.

Use the Insert⇨Footnote command to create a footnote.

View⇨Form

This command changes the database to the form view, where you can view one database record at a time.

Minimum mouse motion

Hot key hysteria

Ample info

You use the Works database form view to enter data in a database.

Extra info

You enter database data with a database form or list.

You can either use the View➪List command to enter data in a Works database, or you can enter data by creating a predesigned form using the File➪WorksWizard command.

View➪Format for Printer

When selected, this command displays a database form in a window that simulates what it looks like when printed. Selecting the View➪Format for Printer command again turns off the display feature.

Extra info

Because some colors look the same as others when printed in black and white, use the View➪Format for Printer option to check your color forms for the correct contrast before you print them with your black and white printer.

Using the File➪Print Preview command shows a color proof of your form, with no regard to what type of printer you have.

View➪Formulas

This command acts like an on/off switch. The *default* position is off. When the command is selected (marked with a check mark), the formulas are visible.

Ample info

When you place formulas in a spreadsheet, choose the View➪Formulas command to make them appear in the cells (as shown in the example). When you select the View➪Formulas command again, the check mark next to the command is removed and the formula's text characters disappear from the cells, but the formulas are still used for your spreadsheet's calculations. This makes the spreadsheet cleaner and easier to follow.

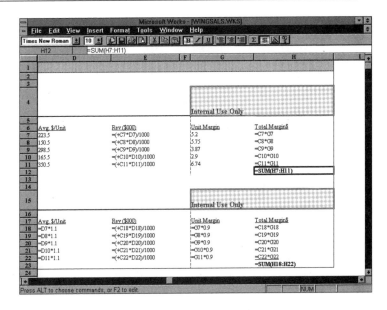

Extra info

You must turn on the formulas to edit them, but you should turn them off when entering the spreadsheet's data.

View⇨Gridlines

This command displays the vertical and horizontal lines of the boundaries that create the cells in a spreadsheet or database list.

Ample info

The default of this command is always on (a check mark is beside the command in the View menu). Choose View⇨Gridlines to turn them off — as shown in the following example.

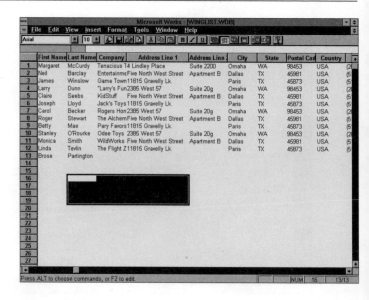

Extra info

Leaving the gridlines on in a spreadsheet or database list allows you to enter data faster and more accurately.

View ⇨ Headers and Footers

This command creates or changes (not displays) the headers and footers in a Works word processor document, spreadsheet, chart, and database list, form, or report.

Ample info

Type the Header and Footer for your document in the Headers and Footers dialog box and then click OK to insert them on every page. If you don't want a header or footer on the first page of your document because it is the title page of the document, click the

No header on 1st page and No footer on 1st page options. To type a header or footer directly on the page, click the Use header and footer paragraphs option and then click OK. Choose Normal or Draft View from the View menu and then type the header's text next to the *H* and the footer's text next to the *F* at the top of your document page. The chevron mark (») that is under the F and H shows the start of the page.

Extra info

To place a date in your header or footer press Ctrl+Shift+; (the Control key, the Shift key, and the semicolon).

You can use any text or paragraph formatting commands when designing headers and footers.

 To change the margin size of a header or footer, use File⇨Page Setup⇨Margins and change the Header and Footer margins in the Page Setup dialog box.

View⇨Hide Record

This command hides the current record in a Works database form or database list.

Ample info

Choose a record you want to hide in a database form or list, and then select the View⇨Hide Record command.

Extra info

 This command hides the data records that you don't want printed or included in form letters, labels, and reports.

 To view the hidden records in a database form or list, use the View⇨Show All Records command.

View⇨List

This command shows the data in a Works database in cells. A column of cells is a database field and a row of cells is a database record.

Minimum mouse motion

Ample info

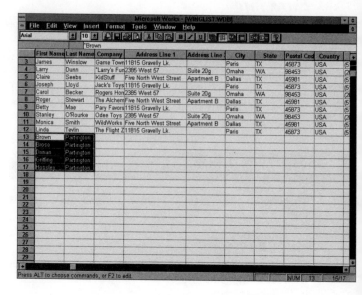

The list view of a database gives you a structured way of changing, deleting, or adding record data to a database.

Extra info

The database list view is a fast way to see all the records' field data in a Works database.

Use the Tools⇨Sort Records command to organize your records in a database.

Using the database form view (View⇨Form or F9) is another way to enter record data in a Works database.

Read Chapter 15 in *Microsoft Works 3 For Windows For Dummies* to learn different ways to enter data in a database.

View ⇨ Normal

This command switches your Works word processor document to the normal view.

Ample info

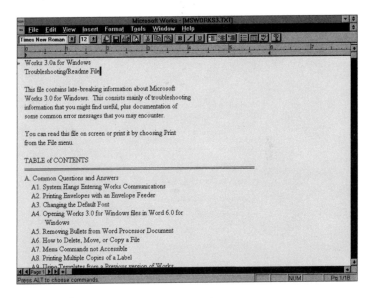

Use this view when you want to see the formatting of the typed text in the word processor and you want inserted objects to be displayed.

Extra info

When designing a layout in a Works word processor document, use the View⇨Page Layout command to show all the page's details.

Remember that the Alt+F+V key combo gives you an accurate preview of your document.

The other two types of view commands in the word processor are View⇨Page Layout and View⇨Draft View.

View⇨Page Layout

Use this word processor command to display the document the same way it looks when it's printed.

Ample info

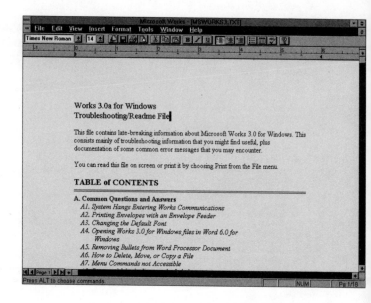

The page layout view is called WYSIWYG (What You See Is What You Get) by computer desktop publishers. You can see all the paragraph formatting, text sizing, objects, headers, and footers, but Works slows down a lot in order to display it all.

Extra info

When working with long documents, use the View⇨Draft to increase display and processing speed.

Use the View⇨Zoom command to magnify your document. This allows you to read the three-point size text at the bottom of legal contract documents.

The other two types of view commands in the word processor are View⇨Normal and View⇨Draft.

View⇨Query

Use this command to switch to the Works database's query view. A query view allows you to find the database records that meet the criteria that you give to the query.

Minimum mouse motion

Ample info

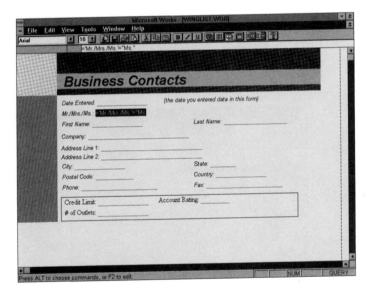

The example query shows all the records that use *Ms.* for salutations in the Mr./Mrs./Ms. field of the database.

Extra info

Use a query to specify which records to merge with a document when using the word processor's Insert⇨Database Field command or the Tools⇨Envelopes and Labels command.

The other views of a Works database are the form, list, and report views.

To create a query, use the Tools⇨Create New Query command.

Read all about database queries in Chapter 17 of *Microsoft Works 3 For Windows For Dummies*.

View⇨Report

Use this database view command to view a database form.

Minimum mouse motion

Ample info

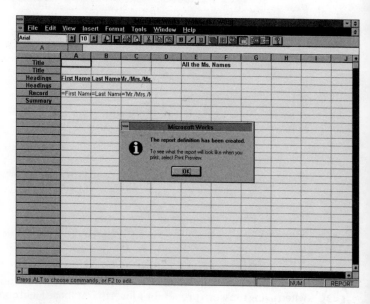

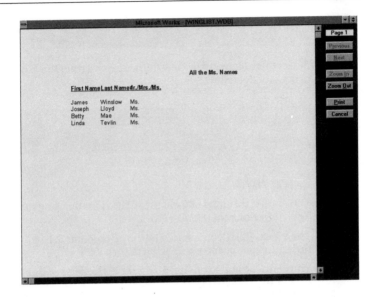

You can use a database form to customize the layout of the data in your database, format it as desired, and then print it. The examples show a simple report using a query for only the *Ms.* salutations criteria in the salutation field of a database. Use the File⇨Print Preview command to see what the form looks like before it is printed.

Extra info

You can use the database report to perform calculations in a certain field — for instance, to add the total amount due on an invoice form.

The other views of a Works database are the form, list, and query views.

To create a database report, use the Tools⇨Create New Report command.

Read all about database queries in Chapter 17 of *Microsoft Works 3 For Windows For Dummies.*

<u>V</u>iew⇨<u>R</u>uler

Select this command to view the horizontal ruler in a Works word processor document.

Extra info

You can set the units of measure in the ruler by using the T<u>o</u>ols⇨<u>O</u>ptions command.

The <u>V</u>iew⇨<u>R</u>uler command is an on/off command. Use it once to turn the ruler on and use it again to turn it off.

You can drag and drop the tab marks in the ruler of the word processor to change their positions. See the Format⇨<u>T</u>abs command for further details.

<u>V</u>iew⇨Show <u>A</u>ll Records

This command shows all the records in a database form or list that were hidden with the <u>V</u>iew⇨Hi<u>d</u>e Record command.

Extra info

Make it a habit to use this command when working with a database. It ensures that you see all the database records.

Use the <u>V</u>iew⇨Hi<u>d</u>e Record command for hiding selected records in your database form or list.

<u>V</u>iew⇨<u>S</u>preadsheet

This command lets you view the spreadsheet of the chart that you are currently editing.

 ### *Extra info*

To view a spreadsheet's chart, use the View⇨Chart command.

View⇨Switch Hidden Records

Using this command in a database makes all hidden records visible and all visible records hidden.

 ### *Extra info*

To hide a record in a database list or form, use the View⇨Hide Record command.

View⇨Toolbar

This command displays the button toolbar of any Works application.

 ### *Extra info*

For speedy work, leave this command on (check marked).

 You can customize the toolbar with the Tools⇨Customize Toolbar command.

View⇨Wrap for Window

This command makes long text lines wrap to the left edge of the current window in the word processor.

Extra info

 Use this command when you have two documents whose windows are *tiled*. This command prevents lines of text from disappearing at the right side of the word processor's window.

 To tile the open documents in Works, use the Window⇨Tile command.

View⇨Zoom

Use this command to zoom in on any Works document.

Ample info

Click a Magnification level from the Zoom dialog box or type a
<u>C</u>ustom one. Click OK to complete the zoom. You may need to
use a high magnification when working with very small text in a
document — like the four-point text used at the bottom of
insurance papers.

Extra info

Use the vertical and horizontal *scroll bars* to move around the
document when it is magnified at a high level.

Window⇨Arrange Icons

When all your Works documents are minimized and scattered
about, use this command to line them up at the bottom of the
window.

Before <u>W</u>indow⇨<u>A</u>rrange Icons:

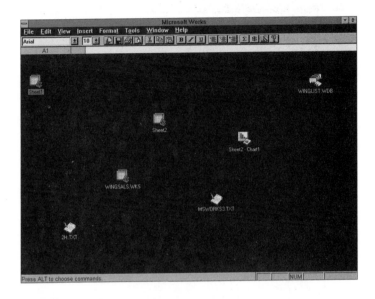

After <u>W</u>indow⇨<u>A</u>rrange Icons:

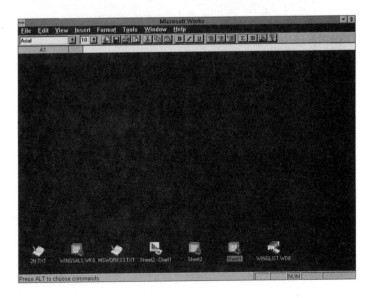

Window⇨Cascade

This command displays the document windows in Works like a
fanned deck of cards.

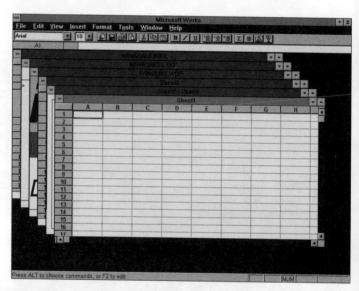

Window⇨Tile

This command displays the open documents of Works side by
side, with no window overlapping another window.

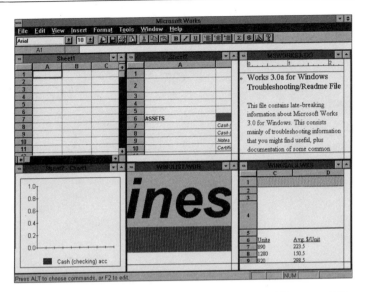

Window⇨Split

This command splits the active window into four separate scrollable parts. This allows you to see the left edge of a document and at the same time view the extreme right edge of the same document.

Drag the window's split bars with your mouse to size the windows to fit your needs.

Extra info

Use this command to view only the important parts of a wide spreadsheet, large form, or long document.

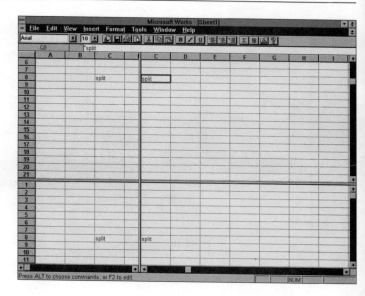

Part III

A Toolbar Cross-Reference

The Word Processor Toolbar

Font Drop-Down List: Click the down arrow to choose a different font from the scrolling drop-down list.

Font Size Drop-Down List: Click the down arrow to choose a different font size from the scrolling drop-down list.

Startup Dialog: Takes you to the Startup dialog box.

The button's menu equivalents: File➪Create New File, File➪WorksWizards, or File➪Templates

Save: Save your document file quickly and often by clicking this button.

The button's menu equivalents: File➪Save or File➪Save As

The button's hot key equivalent: Ctrl+S

Print: Print without that annoying Print dialog box. This button uses the last settings of the Print dialog box.

The button's menu equivalent: File➪Print

The button's hot key equivalent: Ctrl+P

Print Preview: Check out the printed page on your screen before wasting all that paper.

The button's menu equivalent: File⇨Print Preview

Cut: Cuts the selected item from the page and stores it in the Windows Clipboard.

The button's menu equivalent: Edit⇨Cut

The button's hot key equivalent: Ctrl+X

Copy: Copies the selected item from the page and stores it in the Windows Clipboard.

The button's menu equivalent: Edit⇨Copy

The button's hot key equivalent: Ctrl+C

Paste: Pastes the contents of the Windows Clipboard into your document.

The button's menu equivalent: Edit⇨Paste

The button's hot key equivalent: Ctrl+V

Bold: Makes the selected characters bold.

The button's menu equivalent: Format⇨Font and Style⇨Bold

The button's hot key equivalent: Ctrl+B

Italic: Makes the selected characters italic.

The button's menu equivalent: Format⇨Font and Style⇨Italic

The button's hot key equivalent: Ctrl+I

Underline: Underlines the selected characters.

The button's menu equivalent: Format⇨Font and Style⇨Underline

The button's hot key equivalent: Ctrl+U

Left Align: Aligns the selected paragraph with the left margin of the page.

The button's menu equivalent: Format⇨Paragraph⇨Indents and Alignment⇨Left

The button's hot key equivalent: Ctrl+L

Center Align: Aligns the selected paragraph with the center of the page margins.

The button's menu equivalent: Format⇨Paragraph⇨Indents and Alignment⇨Center

The button's hot key equivalent: Ctrl+E

Right Align: Aligns the selected paragraph with the right page margin.

The button's menu equivalent: Format⇨Paragraph⇨Indents and Alignment⇨Right

The button's hot key equivalent: Ctrl+R

Bullets: Adds bullets to the selected paragraphs.

The button's menu equivalent: Format⇨Paragraph⇨Indents and Alignment⇨Bulleted

Insert Table: Inserts a table at the current cursor page position.

The button's menu equivalent: Insert⇨Spreadsheet/Table

Spell Checker: Checks the spelling of the current open document.

The button's menu equivalent: Tools⇨Spelling

Learning Works: Opens the Learning Works dialog box.

The button's menu equivalent: The Help menu

The Spreadsheet Toolbar

Font Drop-Down List: Click the down arrow to choose a different font from the scrolling drop-down list.

Font Size Drop-Down List: Click the down arrow to choose a different font size from the scrolling drop-down list.

Startup Dialog: Takes you to the Startup dialog box.

The button's menu equivalents: File⇨Create New File, File⇨WorksWizards, or File⇨Templates

Save: Save your file quickly and often by clicking this button.

The button's menu equivalents: File⇨Save or File⇨Save As

The button's hot key equivalent: Ctrl+S

Print: Print without that annoying Print dialog box. This button uses the last settings of the Print dialog box.

The button's menu equivalent: File⇨Print

The button's hot key equivalent: Ctrl+P

Print Preview: Check the layout of the spreadsheet on-screen before printing.

The button's menu equivalent: File⇨Print Preview

Cut: Cuts the selected item(s) from the cell or sheet and stores it in the Windows Clipboard.

The button's menu equivalent: <u>E</u>dit⇨Cu<u>t</u>
The button's hot key equivalent: Ctrl+X

Copy: Copies the selected item(s) from the cell or sheet and stores it in the Windows Clipboard.

The button's menu equivalent: <u>E</u>dit⇨<u>C</u>opy
The button's hot key equivalent: Ctrl+C

Paste: Pastes the contents of the Windows Clipboard into the cell or sheet.

The button's menu equivalent: <u>E</u>dit⇨<u>P</u>aste
The button's hot key equivalent: Ctrl+V

Bold: Makes the selected characters bold.

The button's menu equivalent: Forma<u>t</u>⇨<u>F</u>ont and Style⇨<u>B</u>old
The button's hot key equivalent: Ctrl+B

Italic: Makes the selected characters italic.

The button's menu equivalent: Forma<u>t</u>⇨<u>F</u>ont and Style⇨<u>I</u>talic
The button's hot key equivalent: Ctrl+I

Underline: Underlines the selected characters.

The button's menu equivalent: Forma_t_⇨_F_ont and Style⇨_U_nderline

The button's hot key equivalent: Ctrl+U

Left Align: Aligns the selected cell contents with the left border of the cell.

The button's menu equivalent: Forma_t_⇨_P_aragraph⇨_I_ndents and Alignment⇨_L_eft

The button's hot key equivalent: Ctrl+L

Center Align: Aligns the selected cell contents with the center of the cell.

The button's menu equivalent: Forma_t_⇨_P_aragraph⇨_I_ndents and Alignment⇨_C_enter

The button's hot key equivalent: Ctrl+E

Right Align: Aligns the selected cell contents with the right border of the cell.

The button's menu equivalent: Forma_t_⇨_P_aragraph⇨_I_ndents and Alignment⇨_R_ight

The button's hot key equivalent: Ctrl+R

Autosum: Adds the contents of the chosen row or column of cells.

The button's menu equivalent: _I_nsert⇨_F_unction⇨_F_unctions⇨SUM

Currency: Applies the currency format to the selected cell(s) of the sheet.

The button's menu equivalent: Format⇨Number⇨Currency

New Chart: Opens the charting accessory and creates a chart of your choice from the selected cells' data.

Learning Works: Opens the Learning Works dialog box.

The button's menu equivalent: The Help menu

The Spreadsheet Charting Toolbar

Font Drop-Down List: Click the down arrow to choose a different font from the scrolling drop-down list.

Font Size Drop-Down List: Click the arrow to choose a different font size from the scrolling drop-down list.

Startup Dialog: Will take you to the Startup dialog box.

The button's menu equivalents: File⇨Create New File, File⇨WorksWizards, or File⇨Templates

Save: Save your chart quickly and often by clicking this button.

The button's menu equivalents: File⇨Save or File⇨Save As

The button's hot key equivalent: Ctrl+S

Print: Print the chart without that annoying Print dialog box. This button uses the last settings of the Print dialog box.

The button's menu equivalent: File⇨Print

The button's hot key equivalent: Ctrl+P

Print Preview: Check out the looks of the chart on your screen before printing.

The button's menu equivalent: File⇨Print Preview

Copy: Copies the selected item(s) and puts it in the Windows Clipboard.

The button's menu equivalent: Edit⇨Copy

The button's hot key equivalent: Ctrl+C

Bar Chart : Displays a bar chart.

The button's menu equivalent: Gallery⇨Bar

Line Chart: Displays a line chart.

The button's menu equivalent: Gallery⇨Line

Pie Chart: Displays a pie chart.

The button's menu equivalent: Gallery⇨Pie

Scatter Chart: Displays a scatter chart.

The button's menu equivalent: Gallery⇨X-Y (Scatter)

Mixed Chart: Displays a mixed chart.

The button's menu equivalent: Gallery⇨Combination

3-D Area Chart: Displays a 3-D area chart.

The button's menu equivalent: Gallery⇨3-D Area

3-D Bar Chart: Displays a 3-D bar chart.

The button's menu equivalent: Gallery⇨3-D Bar

3-D Line Chart: Displays a 3-D line chart.

The button's menu equivalent: Gallery⇨3-D Li_n_e

3-D Pie Chart: Displays a 3-D pie chart.

The button's menu equivalent: Gallery⇨3-D Pi_e_

Go To 1st Series: Click to go to and select the first chart series in the sheet.

The button's menu equivalent: Edit⇨Legend/Series Labels⇨1st Value Series

Learning Works: Opens the Learning Works dialog box.

The button's menu equivalent: The Help menu

The Database Toolbar

Font Drop-Down List: Click the down arrow to choose a different font from the scrolling drop-down list.

Font Size Drop-Down List: Click the down arrow to choose a different font size from the scrolling drop-down list.

Startup Dialog: Takes you to the Startup dialog box.

The button's menu equivalents: File⇨Create New File,
File⇨WorksWizards, or File⇨Templates

Save: Save your data files quickly and often by clicking this
button.

The button's menu equivalents: File⇨Save or File⇨Save As
The button's hot key equivalent: Ctrl+S

Print: Print data without that annoying Print dialog box. This
button uses the last settings of the Print dialog box.

The button's menu equivalent: File⇨Print
The button's hot key equivalent: Ctrl+P

Print Preview: Check out the page on your screen before printing it.

The button's menu equivalent: File⇨Print Preview

Cut: Cuts the selected item from the page and stores it in the
Windows Clipboard.

The button's menu equivalent: <u>E</u>dit⇨Cu<u>t</u>
The button's hot key equivalent: Ctrl+X

Copy: Copies the selected item from the page and stores it in the Windows Clipboard.

The button's menu equivalent: <u>E</u>dit⇨<u>C</u>opy
The button's hot key equivalent: Ctrl+C

Paste: Pastes the contents of the Windows Clipboard into your document.

The button's menu equivalent: <u>E</u>dit⇨<u>P</u>aste
The button's hot key equivalent: Ctrl+V

Bold: Makes the selected characters bold.

The button's menu equivalent: Forma<u>t</u>⇨<u>F</u>ont and Style⇨<u>B</u>old
The button's hot key equivalent: Ctrl+B

Italic: Makes the selected characters italic.

The button's menu equivalent: Forma<u>t</u>⇨<u>F</u>ont and Style⇨<u>I</u>talic
The button's hot key equivalent: Ctrl+I

Underline: Underlines the selected characters.

The button's menu equivalent: Format⇨Font and Style⇨Underline

The button's hot key equivalent: Ctrl+U

Form View: Switches you to the form view.

The button's menu equivalent: View⇨Form

The button's hot key equivalent: F9

List View: Switches you to the list screen view.

The button's menu equivalent: View⇨List

Query View: Switches you to the query view.

The button's menu equivalent: View⇨Query

Report View: Displays the report view.

The button's menu equivalent: View⇨Report

Insert Field: Inserts a field.

The button's menu equivalent: Insert⇨Record/Field

Insert Record: Inserts a new record.

The button's menu equivalent: Insert⇨Record/Field

Learning Works: Opens the Learning Works dialog box.

The button's menu equivalent: The Help menu

The Communications Toolbar

Startup Dialog: Takes you to the Startup dialog box.

The button's menu equivalents: File⇨Create New File,
File⇨WorksWizards, or File⇨Templates

Save: Save your file quickly and often by clicking this button.

The button's menu equivalents: File⇨Save or File⇨Save As
The button's hot key equivalent: Ctrl+S

Copy: Copies the selected item and stores it in the Windows
Clipboard.

The button's menu equivalent: Edit⇨Copy
The button's hot key equivalent: Ctrl+C

Paste: Pastes the contents of the Windows Clipboard into your text.

The button's menu equivalent: Edit⇨Paste
The button's hot key equivalent: Ctrl+V

Communications Settings: Changes the communications settings.

The button's menu equivalent: Settings⇨Communication

Terminal Settings: Changes the terminal settings.

The button's menu equivalent: Settings⇨Terminal

Phone Settings: Changes the phone settings.

The button's menu equivalent: Settings⇨Phone

Transfer Settings: Changes the transfer settings.

The button's menu equivalent: Settings⇨Transfer

8-N-1 Settings: Changes the communication settings to 8 data bits
with no parity and 1 stop bit.

The button's menu equivalent:
Settings⇨Communications⇨Alt+N+8+1+o

7-E-1 Settings: Changes the communication settings to 7 data bits
with even parity and 1 stop bit.

The button's menu equivalent:
Settings⇨Communications⇨Alt+E+7+1+o

Easy Connect: Dials the current phone number or makes a phone reconnection.

The button's menu equivalent: Phone⇨Easy Connect

Dial/Hangup: Dials the current phone number or hangs up the present connection.

The button's menu equivalent: Phone⇨Dial or Phone⇨Hangup

Pause: Pauses the communications.

The button's menu equivalent: Phone⇨Pause

Capture Text: Captures (saves) the text to be received.

The button's menu equivalent: Tools⇨Capture Text

Send Text: Sends text out.

The button's menu equivalent: Tools⇨Send Text

Send Binary File: Sends a binary file out.

The button's menu equivalent: Tools⇨Send File

Receive Binary File: Click this button to receive a binary file.

The button's menu equivalent: Tools⇨Receive File

Learning Works: Opens the Learning Works dialog box.

The button's menu equivalent: The Help menu

The WordArt Toolbar

Text Template Shape Drop-Down List: Opens a pictorial drop-down list of predefined text-shaping templates.

Font Drop-Down List: Click the down arrow to choose a different font from the scrolling drop-down list.

WordArt Font Size Drop-Down List: Click the down arrow to the right of the drop-down list box to select a specific font's size rather than have the text fit the text area in the best way possible.

Bold: Makes the selected characters bold.

The button's menu equivalent: Format⇨<u>F</u>ont and Style⇨<u>B</u>old
The button's hot key equivalent: Ctrl+B

Italic: Makes the selected characters italic.

The button's menu equivalent: Forma<u>t</u>⇨<u>F</u>ont and Style⇨<u>I</u>talic
The button's hot key equivalent: Ctrl+I

Level Text Height: Makes all the characters an even height.

Turn 90 Degrees: Turns each character 90 degrees counterclockwise.

Stretch to Frame: Stretches all the characters to fit the frame.

The button's menu equivalent: Forma<u>t</u>⇨Stretch to <u>F</u>rame

Text Alignment: Click to select the text alignment you desire from the pop-up menu.

Adjust Character Spacing: Adjusts the spacing between the characters.

The button's menu equivalent: Format⇨Spacing Between Character

Text Rotate: Rotates all the text.

The button's menu equivalent: Format⇨Rotation And Effects

Text Shading: Click to select a pattern and color for the text's foreground and background.

The button's menu equivalent: Format⇨Shading

Text Shadow: Click to select a drop shadow style.

The button's menu equivalent: Format⇨Shadow

Format Border: Click to change the color and the weight of the text's outline.

The button's menu equivalent: Format⇨Border

Part IV

Glossary

Alignment: A term to describe the placement of text between the page margins. Text can be aligned left, center, or right.

Alt Key Combos: A combination of keystrokes that correspond to the underlined keys in menus, commands, and dialog box options.

Bookmarks: Hidden markers you create in a word processor document to help you find a position within your document quickly.

Break Signal: A special data signal sent to another computer during a communications session to alert it to pay attention to your signals instead of its own.

Category: A related group of values positioned along the X (horizontal) axis.

Cell: A box in a spreadsheet or database list that holds values, formulas, or data. The cell's location is named from the intersection of its column label and its row label.

Chart: A visual way of using bars, dots, lines, and other images to show the relationships among data.

Clicking: Pressing the left mouse button and then releasing it. (Named after the clicking sound the mouse makes.)

Communications Program: A Works program that controls your modem and computer to send the proper data through a phone line.

Control Box: A small, button-like box that is located at the upper-left corner of every open window.

Data Labels: The labels used to show the value of a series.

Database Form: A displayed form layout, used to enter data into a database.

Database: A collection of data that has been sorted into records (rows) with descriptive fields (columns).

Default: The initial setting of software.

Dialog Boxes: Appear in your program so that more information, options, and data can be added, changed, or chosen.

Double-Clicking: When you press the left mouse button twice in rapid succession.

Downloading: When you are receiving data from a computer that you're connected to during a communications session.

Dragging: When you select or highlight something in your program — then move it by moving your mouse while its left mouse button is still pressed.

Drawing Program: A drawing program uses vectors, polygons, and color fills to create art.

Droplines: Are vertical lines that line up with each point on the horizontal (X) axis of an area chart and help contrast its categories.

Electricity: The stuff your computer eats that's provided by the Power Company.

Electronic Mail: The digital files that are sent to someone using a telephone modem or a networked computer system.

Elevator Shaft: The part of the scroll bar that the scroll box moves in.

Ellipses: Selecting a command with an ellipses suffix (...) always brings up a dialog box in your program's window.

Embedded: When an object is embedded, it can be double-clicked in order to open the original program that created it.

Field Entry: The blank areas in a database form or report.

Field Lines: The lines under the field entries in a database form or report.

Field Names: The names given to fields in a database, which can be seen at the top of each column in a database list.

Field Summary Row: A row in a database report that shows a calculation performed in the report or the total amount of records in it.

Fields: A descriptive component of a database that is displayed in columns in the database list view.

File Name Extension: The three text characters following the period in a file name.

Form View: A database view that allows you to enter records in a database one at a time.

Gridlines: Are vertical and horizontal lines used in spreadsheets, lists, and charts to help you view its contents.

Highlighting: Selecting information in your document using mouse or keyboard techniques. Once highlighted, the selected content's color changes — thus the name *highlight*.

Hot Keys: The keystroke alternatives on the right side of a drop-down menu for the command on the left side.

Hot Pants: Historic garments worn by men and women — circa 1970.

Legend: A descriptive list of what the colors, fills, or patterns mean in the series of a chart.

Linked: When an object in a document is linked, the original content of the object's file can be changed and the changes will be reflected in the linked object when the document is opened later.

List View: The view in the database for listing data in cells. A column of cells is a *field* and a row of cells is a *record*.

Logarithmic: An axes scaling that allows for high series value differences to be displayed in a chart.

Marquee: When you drag your mouse to form a rectangular box on the screen that flashes like an old movie theater sign.

Menu Bar: The horizontal bar that contains the menu titles.

Menu Special: A cheap lunch!

Modem: A small electronic computer attachment that connects your computer to a telephone line for the purpose of connecting two computers together.

Network: A group of computers that are hooked together so that their users can share information, programs, and equipment.

Note-It: A Works accessory that electronically posts those little stick-it notes to your documents.

Off-line: When you're *not* connected to another computer in a communication session.

On-line: When you *are* connected to another computer in a communication session.

Painting Program: A computer program that uses the collection of small, colored dots to create an image.

Pointing: Moving your mouse so that your screen cursor moves to the desired location in a program.

Print Area: A group of cells selected for printing from a spreadsheet.

Quadruple-Clicking: A good way to get carpal tunnel syndrome.

Query View: Shows only the records that match your set of conditions. Only the data that matches the query will display or print in a database report.

Range Name: A name given to a group of cells in a database list or spreadsheet.

Record: Holds the collection of field data in a database. A record is one row of cells in a database list.

Report (database): A database view that shows how the data will be placed when printed.

Right-Clicking: When you press the right mouse button and then release it.

Script: A text file created when parts of a communications session are recorded.

Scroll Arrows: A set of arrows on the ends of a scroll bar that allow you to move around a window in short increments when clicked.

Scroll Bars: Moves you around to see the hidden portions of a crowded window when clicked.

Scroll Box: Dragging this part of the scroll bar will move you around a crowded window in large increments.

Selecting: You select information in your document using mouse or keyboard techniques. See *Highlighting*.

Series: A group of related items arranged along a scaled axis.

Sign-on: The initial name, password, and other data entries given to a computer service to get into its system.

Snap to Grid: A tool used to keep things aligned and spaced evenly in a database form.

Snap, Crackle, Pop: The sound your computer makes when you spill a soft drink on the keyboard.

Spell Checker: An accessory in Works that checks a word processor document, spreadsheet, or database form for misspellings.

Spreadsheet: An X, Y table that allows the user to define relationships (mathematical and logical) between the rows, columns, and cells.

Standard Deviation: Formula used for population calculations by tax collectors.

Startup Dialog Box: The first dialog box that appears when you start the Works program.

Status Bar: The bar that is usually displayed at the bottom of your open program's window; it contains various program information.

Tab: Adjustable points in the width of a page that text can be aligned under.

Template: A document with lots of styles, designs, and layouts for you to start with.

Thumbnail: A very small, postage stamp-like graphic.

Tiled: Spaced side-by-side without overlapping one another.

Title Bar: The horizontal strip at the top of any window, dialog box, program, or working document.

Toolbar Buttons: The icon command buttons in a toolbar.

Toolbar: Filled with toolbar buttons, it lies under the menu bar, which makes this bar the third from the top.

Transfer Protocol: The type of programming code used to transfer data from one computer to another in a communications session.

Triple-Clicking: When you press the left mouse button three times in rapid succession.

Uploading: Sending data to another computer in a communications session.

Variance: The difference between two values.

Word Processor: A computer program that is dedicated to the layout of words, sentences, and paragraphs.

WordArt: A program that allows you to shape and mold text to form unique typographical designs.

Workspace: Is the term given for the positions and sizes of all of the open documents in a Microsoft Works application.

Zeldoni: The inventor of the small rubber feet located on the bottom of all computer equipment.

Index

• O •

objects
    creating/inserting, 112
    editing linked, 31–32
    linking, 30–31
    sending to back, 73
    sizing, 69–70
on-line help, 93–96
Open dialog box, 11, 41
Options dialog box, 145

• P •

page breaks, 113
    inserting, 102
page layout view, 168
Page Setup dialog box, 42–43
Paginate (F9) key, 146
Paragraph dialog box, 64–66
paragraphs
    formatting, 64–67
    hyphenation, 142–143
Paste Series dialog box, 33–34
Paste Special dialog box, 34
Patterns and Colors dialog box, 69
Patterns dialog box, 68
Phone⇨Break command, 119
Phone⇨Dial Again command, 120
Phone⇨Dial command, 119–120
Phone⇨Easy Connect command,
    120–121
Phone⇨Pause command, 121–122
phone, settings, 124
Picture/Object dialog box, 69–70
pictures
    sizing, 69–70
    thumbnail form, 14
pie chart, 88–89
pointing, 4
Print dialog box, 44
Print Preview window, 45
Printer Setup dialog box, 46
printers, configuring, 46
printing
    page setup, 44–45
    previewing, 45–46

programs
    chart accessory, 15
    ClipArt Gallery, 13–14
    Communications, 15
    component parts, 10–16
    exiting, 41
    Microsoft Draw, 14–15, 104–105
    Note-It, 13, 111
    spell checker, 16
    WordArt, 14, 117–119
Protection dialog box, 70–71

• Q •

Query (F3) key, 156
query view, 169–170
query
    applying, 156
    deleting, 134–135
    duplicate, 137
    naming, 144
    new, 131–132

• R •

radar chart, 89–90
Range Name dialog box, 113
ranges, naming, 113–114
Recalculate (F9) key, 128
Receive File dialog box, 147–148
Record Script dialog box, 148
records
    adding, 114–115
    copying, 21–22
    cutting to Clipboard, 23
    deleting current, 102–103
    deleting selected, 103
    hiding, 165
    selecting, 37
    setting height, 71–72
    showing all, 172
    sorting, 151–152
    viewing, 161–162
    viewing hidden, 173
rectangles, inserting into forms, 115
Rename Script dialog box, 139
Replace dialog box, 36

• U •

• V •

❏ **YES!**

Please keep me informed about IDG's World
of Computer Knowledge. Send me the latest
IDG Books catalog.